FACE READING

What does your face say?

by

Barbara Roberts

ISBN: 0-9642727-0-9

First Edition: September 1994
Printed in the United States of America

To order this book, contact:

Barbara Roberts
#227-1106 2nd St.
Encinitas, CA 92024
(619) 944-1460

ACKNOWLEDGMENTS

I would like to personally thank all those who have so generously contributed of their love, time and energy to this manual!

Dr. Narayan Singh, International teacher and author, who has spent over 25 years developing the accurate psychological interpretations of various facial features and who was the first to train me in Face Reading. Thank you, Narayan, with deep gratitude.

Dr. Narayan Singh sells his books and can be contacted at: 708 Mohawk Drive, #18 Boulder, Colorado 80303 (Phone: 303-499-1512)

**Photos: Front cover: Jeré Piper (Photographer: Bruce Rogers), Jessica Garcia, Javier Ramos, and Jon Connor. Back cover : Author photographed by 2nd Street Photography.

Editor: Andrew Freedman
Design & Layout: Robert Donnelly
Cover layout: *Headline Graphics*, Encinitas, CA.

And my friends whose loving smiles are featured in this manual: (in order of appearance)

1. Marsha Lipton

2. Curt Johnson (Photographer: Dave Ferris)

3. Tamlin Pavelsky

4. Jeré Piper

5. Martha Odegaard

6. Sara Madden-Connor (self-portrait)

7. Kayoko Yoshikai

8. Mekayla Reitz

9. Thelma Brown (Photographer: 2nd Street Photography, Encinitas)

10. Sara and Rachael Madden-Connor (Photographer: Sara Madden-Connor)

11. Jessica Garcia and Javier Ramos

12. Nancy and Ben Johnson (Photographer: 2nd Street Photography, Encinitas)

13. Jon Connor and Jonas Madden-Connor (Photographer: Sara Madden-Connor)

14. Debbie Ashton and Addie Stoller

15. Dolores and Joe Sasway

16. Therese Madden-Connor and Jon Connor (Photographer: Sara Madden-Connor)

* * * * *

And special personal thanks to my friends from the "InSide San Diego" TV Show (Laura Buxton, Amielle Moyer, Vicki Gloor), and thanks for your personal support: (In alphabetical order) Kathleen Burt, Mary Jane Frahm, Arbutus and Raymond Fricke, Kathleen Krudy, Kathy and Rick Link, Suzanne O'Neal, Jim Roberts, Sylvia Stern, and Pauline Wright.

PREFACE

Face Reading is an ancient system of inner awareness, a way of seeing that which is *special* in each face and in each soul. In every face we find an expression of hidden potentials and unique gifts. In the true understanding of facial features, which goes beyond superficial features or ethnic traits, there is an unfolding of an *inner* mystery that draws each of us into an underlying kinship with each other. Let us look to the beauty of each face, seeing there in a *spark* of the Divine.

TABLE OF CONTENTS

TABLE OF CONTENTS

INTRODUCTION

HOW I BECAME INTERESTED IN FACE READING

When I was twenty, I read my first book on Face Reading and was fascinated to learn that the mental, emotional, and financial life ahead of me might already be recorded in the features of my face! Just out of college, I was eager to grow, change, and manifest my true potential—if only I could figure out what it was! In Face Reading I discovered a <u>system</u> of understanding human nature that cut across cultural, geographical, ethnic, gender and age differences, enabling me to look deeply into myself and other people. In reviewing the 200 or so books and articles published on Face Reading, I found to my consternation that most of the authorities unfortunately disagreed, contradicting each other in their interpretations of the same facial feature. I didn't know who or what to believe, and there seemed to be no one who could teach me how to practice this system "live," with real people. Then one day while working in clinical medical research, I attended a class taught by Dr. Narayan Singh, author and international teacher of Face Reading.

At the time of our meeting, my father was dying, and I was searching and grasping for ways to make peace with him before he passed on. I needed lots of healing and understanding and was coming up short! Having just met Dr. Singh, I approached him with a photo of my dad. Handing it to him, I mutely stood before him.

"Your father was an orphan, wasn't he?" he started.

I nodded, my mouth agape, as he analyzed my father's character in depth. He helped me for the first time to understand my father as the person he truly was—a man with his own gifts, longings, and emotional wounds. It was this insight that gave me peace with him before he died. And that awareness propelled me forward to study Face Reading in depth.

Dr. Singh's extensive writings encompass both the psychological meanings of facial features and a way of understanding the right and left sides of the face. His unique gift and interest lie in the latter, the "Intuitive" approach (outlined in Part I of this book). This is the focus of his classes. For me, the fun and creativity comes in accurately analyzing a person's character from the hundreds of "facial features." After years of study and seeing hundreds of faces in both classes and individual sessions, I have developed my own system for reading the face. This "how-to" manual outlines that system for a beginner and includes:

- 80+ Drawings of the most common facial features.

- Psychological meanings of each facial feature (Drawings, Part II) which have been validated by a minimum of 20 people with that particular feature.

- A practical, universal approach to understanding these ancient teachings--accurate for people of different ages, genders and ethnic backgrounds.

- An intuitive and spiritual approach to reading the face.

- A method for combining the individual facial features into a whole.

- How to say what you see: Attitudinal guidelines for sensitive communication.

- Relationships: What we can learn from each other. How to look at a couple to see if they are compatible. Brother-sister, husband-wife, mother-son, sisters. Personal face readings of life lessons and areas of growth.

- Worksheets in each section for experiential learning with a partner.

- Individual face readings of real people.

STORIES THE FACE CAN TELL

The following are some of the true stories of people I have met in my years doing hundreds of Face Readings. They illustrate how to integrate or "weave" the various facial features.

EARS "OUT": MUSICAL ABILITY "IN"

The ears are a sensitive barometer of how we tune in to the Big picture of what is going on around us. When the ears come forward, away from the head as they do with Prince Charles or Ross Perot, the person will be either very unconventional in their behavior, a "maverick" and/or they will have musical ability. The ears in a forward position allows them to more sensitively pick up sounds, which explains the natural gift for music. (To try this yourself: While a friend is talking, place your hands behind your ears and push them forward, continuing to listen to the person speak. When the ears are forward, you will notice that you can hear the speaker better. Now let your ears relax, and you will notice that the person's voice will seem to recede in volume.)

When the left ear comes forward, the person will be a natural at singing, rhythm or playing an instrument, and this gift will often be a hobby. If the right ear comes forward, the person will often be drawn to perform music professionally.

I once asked a mother what her three year old son's interests were, noticing that his forward left ear indicated music as a perfect outlet. I suggested she get him a drum set. "I can't!" she replied in astonishment. "We already gave him one last year, and that's his favorite toy!"

BLUE-GREY EYES: THE INTRIGUE AND THE HUMANITY

Several years ago I was invited to a private party to read the faces of some wealthy women in a suburb where the guest houses looked as though they were from the TV show, *"The Lifestyles of the Rich and Famous."* As I entered a lush setting of overhanging gardens with flowing fountains, I was greeted and ushered into the Persian-carpeted study to set up my work. Outside the door, a woman with blonde hair and blue-grey eyes was in a frenzy, fussing at the kitchen staff about the inappropriate size of the croissants and their fillings. She spoke quickly in French, then Spanish. Pushing forward into the study to meet me, she extended her hand cordially, and I thought, "I wonder what I can say that will be useful to this woman?"

While she stretched out on the satin couch awaiting her Face Reading, I looked intently into her face. She nodded as I said various things about her face and character. Then I focused on her blue-grey eyes. Their particular steely-grey color (a color which I always associate with Sherlock Holmes), creates an analytical, clear-thinking and unemotional gaze. A person with this color of grey is fooled by no one and is impressed by only the finest in quality. Specifically, the blue-hue overtone is seen in people who have a spiritual interest in serving humanity privately or anonymously. I mumbled something to her about doing selfless, humanitarian work, thinking that I was making a fool of myself because this seemed absurd! Startled, she drew back and whispered, "Turn off the tape."

Then she leaned forward and said, "What I do all day is make and deliver meals for AIDS patients in this area. Only my husband knows that."

We smiled at each other and sat in silence.

"TEACHER LINES"

Craving a chocolate yogurt, I waltzed into a local frozen yogurt shop. For several minutes I watched the four women scurrying behind the counter helping the noon-hour customers. One of them seemed as though she didn't fit into the picture. It reminded me of those childhood puzzle drawings in which one of the ducks looked different from the other three. Looking more closely at her face as I ate my yogurt, I asked, "Excuse me, you are a grade school teacher aren't you?" She had very large cheeks with "teacher lines" on the right side of her face, the "world" side. When she turned to the side, I saw her down-turned nose, a facial feature reflecting financial planning. I continued, "You also own this business, don't you? "Yes," she replied in shock. "I am taking a six-month break from teaching third grade to start this business!"

WHAT VISIBLE GUMS CAN TELL US ABOUT CHARGE CARDS!

When a person smiles and their gum line is apparent above the teeth, this reveals a tendency to not only spend money easily, but also to have a hard time budgeting. The more revealing the gums, the less the person even tries to budget!

Fred and Maggie, a married couple, sat in my living room, both grinning broadly, revealing beautiful teeth with healthy pink gums showing widely above their front teeth. "So," Fred challenged, "I don't know if I buy this Face Reading stuff like Maggie does. What can you tell me about myself?" I countered swiftly, "So, not doing too well with your new budget are you?" The three of us broke out laughing.

THE ROUND BALL ON THE CHIN

A round ball on the chin (with a dimple in it) most often reveals a very strong sex drive or sensual nature.

Sitting with me in my home, Elizabeth was producing one photo after another of her past boyfriends, asking me the nature of the relationships. Which of these men would be the most compatible for her, she wondered? She came to Larry and handed me the picture, smiling as she did so. "So, what about this one, Barbara?" Seeing the ball (and dimple) on the chin as the most pronounced part of his face, I asked, "Was this relationship 98% *physical?*" She leaned forward.

"100%," she laughed.

JUST HORSING AROUND!

A woman with finely-textured blonde hair, sparkling, deep blue eyes, and fine-pored skin sat before me. In my mind I analyzed her features quickly: fine hair shaft, fine-pored skin, deep blue eyes, all features which express *sensitivity*. She is probably so sensitive, in fact, that she has problems being in the mundane world. I checked the jaw/chin area to see the "grit" level in the face, the follow through and willpower, to validate my conclusion. A narrow jaw, combined with the other features, made her face more gentle and chiseled in kindness. In seconds my mind was putting all the cues together: With so many features for sensitivity in her face, I wonder if at times she finds people too abrasive? Would she prefer the company of animals for companionship? If so, what animal would most appeal to her? Animals with gentleness, intelligence, and responsiveness – must be horses. Not missing a beat, I leaned forward. "Do you like horses?" Well, the room broke out into either astonished laughter or gasps. The woman's mouth dropped open, and she managed to get out, "I've loved horses since I was five. I own my own stable. Sometimes I have a hard time functioning in the world, I feel too sensitive for its hardness. Horses help me feel connected to life."

THE MYSTERIES BEHIND "UNUSUAL EARS"

Though the majority of people we see around us have good characters and are trustworthy, Face Reading occasionally reveals dangerous, unusual or eccentric tendencies in a person. Joseph Goebbels, Hitler's World War II Propaganda Minister had very unusually-shaped ears which stuck out from his head at a distinctly odd angle. With his unusual ears, sinister and vacant eyes, his flat, scarred cheeks, this man looked as vicious as he was.

Years ago, a friend, Jane Marie, sat in my living room. Taking out the picture of her brother, she held it in front of me saying, "Barbara, tell me about him." I saw a man of fifty, dressed in a three-piece suit, standing in a busy business setting, looking very official. Everything about him looked affluent except his ears. He had ears like Joseph Goebbels. Though I usually start with a <u>positive</u> quality about person's face, this time I blurted out, "This man has criminal tendencies." Jane Marie's jaw dropped, "How did you know that? Right after this picture was taken, he was arrested for forgery. I think he went to prison, and we never heard from him again."

However, people with unusual ears can also have happy endings. A year or two after Jane Marie came to see me, Louise laid out various photos of her relatives. Holding up baby pictures of her adopted daughter, I again saw the "Goebbels" ears. After birth, the child had been in several temporary homes in which her mother felt she had been abused. A sad-looking baby face with unusual ears looked back at me from the pictures. However, Louise's family so loved and nurtured the little girl that by age 8, her photo revealed a sweet young girl with beautiful ears. Over the years, her ear shape had completely changed!

Part I

The Intuitive Approach

GUIDELINES FOR FACE READING

HOW TO "READ" WITH THE HEART

Before Zen Masters teach techniques of meditation, there is a period of mental and inner preparation so as to enable the student to attune him- or herself to the Spirit of the discipline. Outer skills are imparted only after the inner framework has been laid.

Because Face Reading reveals powerful and intimate information about people who would otherwise be total strangers to us, the following are some suggested Guidelines to help the beginner know "how" and "what" to say in response to the information seen in another's face.

It is important to prepare yourself first to be open and receptive. Before starting a session, I close my eyes and pray briefly for the client, asking that God guide what we say, that it be accurate, healing and useful.

BASIC PRINCIPLES

1. Seek to understand the person you are reading. Be compassionate.

2. The goals of Face Reading as an introspective tool are always *healing and insight.* The person must be able to integrate and understand what for them may be new psychological information. Leave them feeling positive and hopeful about themselves.

3. As a person heals from within and grows in wisdom, the face will reflect this new radiance. The face you are interpreting is like a computer print-out of the emotional, spiritual and mental past. For those clients involved in intensive inner work, the physical transformation may not be obvious immediately—as the soft tissue changes slower than the consciousness!

4. It is important to note that Face Reading as a tool for self-understanding is not a replacement for professional counseling or medical intervention. When particularly painful areas come up, I remind the client of the availability of individual, marital and family counseling, 12-step groups (such as AA, ACA, Coda, NA, etc.), Parent's Effectiveness Training (P.E.T.), prayer and meditation or church group support, assertiveness training or other personal development classes offered at most community colleges.

5. Though accurate and insightful, Face Reading is not a psychic tool in that it does not predict the future. Neither does it seek to give advice about what the client should or should not do.

6. Before beginning with someone who is unfamiliar with Face Reading, explain the Intuitive Approach (Part I). Discuss what different areas of the face signify. Then explain to the person that you will also be psychologically interpreting their facial features. You might show them photos from this book or ones from magazines that illustrate these concepts. I usually start by analyzing the facial features and end with the intuitive approach of dividing the face into quadrants.

HOW TO COMMUNICATE WHAT YOU SEE

1. Be gentle, kind and tactful.

2. Start with a positive attribute and emphasize the client's strengths (i.e., intelligence, sense of humor, determination). Gradually bring up one of their challenges or areas of stress as you see it in their facial features. Always phrase what you say with love. For example, "Are you working right now on issues of 'personal power'?" (positive) rather than, "I see that you are full of rage" (insulting).

3. Allow the client to draw you in. Let them to share their feelings about what you see expressed in their face.

4. Frequently validate your intuitive perceptions by asking, "Is this true about you?" and/ or by asking them to nod "yes" as you go along. If something you are saying is inaccurate, ask that they stop you. Validating your accuracy has a two-fold importance. It gives the client a chance to respond to your accuracy, and it lets you know that the client is understanding and integrating what is being said to them.

5. Always respect the client's sensitive emotional boundaries. Face Reading is not: "I know all about you; you know nothing about me." Nor is it a subtle spiritual or emotional way to manipulate or overwhelm others.

During the reading be alert for changes in the client's body language, which may indicate they are unable to emotionally take in what you are saying. Some indications may be a look of confusion, a sudden crossing of the arms or legs, or a physical move away from you. If you see these, <u>stop</u>! Ask the client to tell you what he or she is experiencing, and ask if he or she wants you to continue.

If you feel they should know something about themselves "for their own good," but you feel they will be overwhelmed emotionally in the process, stop and look at your own motives for insisting that they get it.

6. In an informal group or party setting, say only positive things to a person about their character.

7. And finally, periodically look at your own face in the mirror. It helps keeps one humble!

HOW TO "READ" YOUR <u>OWN</u> FACE
(without heart palpitations!)

Before studying Face Reading, we were probably oblivious to what our facial features meant. After studying, however, we not only understand them, but we may feel a degree of private exasperation, or we may wish for features indicative of stronger personalities or better lifestyles.

"I wish I had a tall, broad forehead," or "I wish my nose were bigger." This could be depressing! We must remind ourselves that just as we see others with compassion, so too must we see our own journey—emotional, spiritual, and physical-- as our *unique* way to understanding and soul realization.

Our face <u>will</u> change as we do inner, meditative, or counseling work to free ourselves from self-doubt, pain, fear, or self-limitation. The area which will most clearly reveal recovery or inner transformation, despite what the other facial features show, is the <u>eye tone.</u> If the <u>Radiance</u> coming from the eyes gives the viewer a feeling of compassion, wisdom, love and joy, then even if all the facial features *appear* negative, there is recovery and spiritual progress being made. And this change in eye tone may override the psychological tendencies suggested by the other facial features. This feeling coming from the eyes is the pivotal point that separates saints from criminals, both of whom have often endured tremendous personal obstacles. The saint has radiance and love pouring from their gaze. The criminal (whose right side of the face may also express the pain and trauma) may have an eye tone which appears flat and cold. When we see paintings of world religious figures, such as Christ, Buddha, Moses, Mohammed, or Krishna, we see and feel a quality of compassion, serenity, calmness and light emanating from their eyes.

Radiance in the eye tone indicates any or all of the following:

a) The person is aware of their shortcomings or life lessons and wishes to work through them, instead of ignoring or denying them.
b) The person is actively working them out.
c) The persons has already worked them out even if the face has not clearly manifested the changes.

The important thing to understand is that when there is Radiance emanating from the eyes, the individual is living more from their soul nature than they are from their psychological personalities, so the emotional ramifications expressed in facial features do not impact the individual as much, nor do they reflect the person's true state of development.

In the ancient Orient there is a story about an Emperor who wanted a painting of the most famous prophet in his realm. He commissioned his best painter to complete the work, and shortly after, the oil painting was unveiled before the whole court. Understanding Face Reading, the Emperor became confused as he looked at the painting. The facial features expressed not a great soul, but a man of very evil nature. Infused with curiosity, the monarch went alone on horseback to meet the man of God. On seeing his face, the Emperor was astounded to realize that the art work had been a perfect rendering.

The wise one, understanding the Emperor's dilemma, explained: "All the evil tendencies you see are expressed in my facial features, but one by one I have battled against these defects of character, transforming them in myself—from evil to good. This is what has given me my strength."

HOW TO "READ" INTUITIVELY

The Intuitive Approach to Face Reading involves dividing the face in half or into four quadrants and then getting a feeling from the area you are viewing. The feelings you perceive might be happiness, sadness, anger, fear, confusion, etc. An easy way to do this is to mentally put your face in the exact expression of the person you are seeing. Then, feel. What are the feelings _you_ experience when your face looks like theirs?

PREPARATION

Use a piece of thick bond paper or cardboard. Fold it in half lengthwise, and then again in half widthwise. You will have a piece of paper with four equal quadrants. Take a scissors and cut along the fold-lines, cutting away one quarter of the paper. You will now have three complete sections remaining. Place this paper in front of your client's face in different positions so you can look individually at each of the four quadrants of his/her face.

THE FOUR QUADRANTS OF THE FACE

In his system of Face Reading, Dr. Narayan Singh divided the human face into two sides: the Right representing the public life or world side and the Left reflecting the private life or "inner child" side:

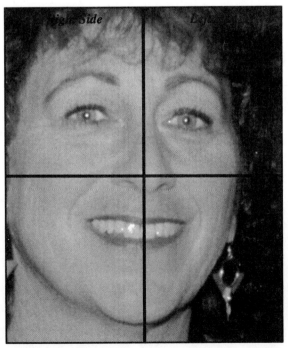

The Right side of our face expresses how fellow-workers, our boss, or our acquaintances will perceive us. As we grow older, it reflects how the world has treated us—success or failure in business, health or illness, divorce, crisis, etc. Essentially, the Right side of our face expresses what has happened _to_ us.

The Left side of our face, on the other hand, represents our spiritual, inner transformation. It is what we've done with what has happened to us. This is the person we are when no one is looking. For dating, getting along with our spouses, finding a job and boss with whom we can be compatible, or understanding our children and parents, looking at the core person expressed on the Left side can be invaluable. This is the true inner person.

Dr. Singh emphasized that to make a reliable and accurate reading of the face, it is vital to clearly orient yourself to the person's Right and Left sides.

The vertical dividing line for the face is the tip of the nose above the nostrils. This point will divide the face into two sections, one from the forehead to the top of the nostrils and the other from the nostrils to the jaw.

In the upper quadrant the cheek area signifies the person's feelings while the right cheek and eye area represents how the person relates, projects and uses feelings to impact the environment. The left cheek and eye area expresses how the person will express their feelings in intimate relationships.

In the lower quadrant, the lips reflect emotional aspects of the person's childhood. The right side of the mouth reveals what the person was told about themselves and the left side of the mouth expresses what they told themselves about what was said <u>to</u> them. If for example, we were told that there were many "should's" in life and there was an atmosphere of control and rigidity in the home, our right mouth will express this tightness. If, on the other hand, other loving adults or teachers gave us positive input about ourselves, then our left mouth will look more relaxed.

WHEN THE RIGHT AND LEFT SIDES OF THE FACE ARE DIFFERENT

1) The Right looks happier, more joyful, more relaxed, or more confident, etc. than the Left side.

An example is a woman who has fascinated art historians for centuries because the two sides of her face reveal completely different people. Da Vinci's *Mona Lisa* is a complex woman whose Right face reflects peace and shyness, creating the image of a salt of the earth mother. Her Left face, on the other hand, with its tightened lip area, suggests cruelty. When an individual's persona (Right side) looks great, but their Left side (who they are inside) reflects sadness or disturbance, this suggests the person is not as happy as they would like their acquaintances to believe them to be. The person may be adjusting to major life losses or dreams which have not come to fruition in the way they had hoped. In Curt's face, the Rock of Gibraltar steadiness expressed on the Right and Left sides reveals integrity with an intense and serious nature. For those of us with that kind of emotional make-up, major changes or crises will express deeply on the face. As we adjust and integrate the changes, the face will again become more peaceful. (see *Figure 1*)

Right Side
"World"

Left Side
"Inner Child"

Figure 1

2) The Left side of the person looks happier, more joyful, more relaxed or more confident, etc. than the Right side.

When the core or inner person appears radiant, it means that despite the difficult outer experiences in life such as divorce, poverty, ill health, abandonment, etc. which are reflected on the Right side, the person has overcome these trials, inwardly transforming themselves. This transformation is usually both emotional and spiritual in nature and manifests in the positive expressions on the Left side of the face. Many of the great saints have traumatic right faces and glowing left faces. It is what is learned and gained from experiences not the experiences themselves that makes the Left side of the face shine. In the photo below (*Figure 2*), Tamlin's Right side reveals a go-getter, curious and eager to master skills in the world. The Left side is more relaxed, and reflects sincerity and warmth. In this case, the two sides are both positive and yet reveal different facets of the same person.

Right Side
"World"

Left Side
"Inner Child"

Figure 2

3) The Left side looks the same as the Right.

This symmetry usually denotes that the person has the same way of responding in public as they do in their private life. With this person, there is a warmth and a genuineness you feel right away. "What you see is what you get." One gets a sense of stability and sincerity when the two facial sides are similar. (see *Figure 3* on the next page)

Right Side
"World"

Left Side
"Inner Child"

Figure 3

PUTTING IT ALL TOGETHER: EXERCISE WITH A PARTNER

THE INTUITIVE APPROACH

Name:_____

Partner's Name:_____

Date:_____

A. RIGHT/LEFT SPLIT Look at your partner (at eye-level) and:

1) Cover the **LEFT** side of their face with your vertically folded cardboard sheet.

2) My *intuitive* feelings about my partner's **RIGHT** side ("World Side") are: (It is sad, joyful, angry, controlled, fearful, content, etc.)

3) Now cover the **RIGHT** side of their face with your vertically folded cardboard sheet.

4) My *intuitive* feelings about my partner's **LEFT** side ("inner child" side) are: (It is sad, joyful, angry, controlled, fearful, content, etc.)

5) **NOTE:** Are the two sides the same or different? (If different, in what areas and in what ways?)

B. LOOKING AT THE FOUR INDIVIDUAL QUADRANTS

Open your cardboard "viewer." Covering the face *completely,* and then exposing only one quadrant at a time, record your *intuitive* perceptions about your partner. (The *bottom tip* of the *nose above the nostrils* is the *horizontal mid-point* of the face. Place the cardboard piece along it for separating the upper and lower quadrants.)

UPPER RIGHT quadrant represents how they see the world.
My *intuitive* feelings about my partner are:

LOWER RIGHT quadrant represents social and family rules, the "shoulds" in their childhood, and what they were told about themselves.
My *intuitive* feelings about my partner are:

UPPER LEFT quadrant represents their self-concept, how they feel about themselves when no one is looking.
My *intuitive* feelings about my partner are:

LOWER LEFT quadrant represents how they feel and express themselves in intimate relationships, and what they told themselves they were like in response to family dynamics.
My *intuitive* feelings about my partner are:

SWITCH

Now take a separate compatibility worksheet and switch partners. Allow the person to look at your face and record their feelings.

THE OTHER PARTNER

Name:_____

Partner's Name:_____

Date:_____

A. RIGHT/LEFT SPLIT Look at your partner (at eye-level) and:

1) Cover the **LEFT** side of their face with your vertically folded cardboard sheet.

2) My *intuitive* feelings about my partner's **RIGHT** side ("World Side") are: (It is sad, joyful, angry, controlled, fearful, content, etc.)

3) Now cover the **RIGHT** side of their face with your vertically folded cardboard sheet.

4) My *intuitive* feelings about my partner's **LEFT** side ("inner child" side) are: (It is sad, joyful, angry, controlled, fearful, content, etc.)

5) **NOTE:** Are the two sides the same or different? (If different, in what areas and in what ways?)

B. LOOKING AT THE <u>FOUR INDIVIDUAL QUADRANTS</u>

Open your cardboard "viewer." Covering the face *completely,* and then exposing only one quadrant at a time, record your *intuitive* perceptions about your partner. (The *bottom tip* of the *nose above the nostrils* is the *horizontal mid-point* of the face. Place the cardboard piece along it for separating the upper and lower quadrants.)

UPPER RIGHT quadrant represents how they see the world.
My *intuitive* feelings about my partner are:

LOWER RIGHT quadrant represents social and family rules, the "shoulds" in their childhood, and what they were told about themselves.
My *intuitive* feelings about my partner are:

UPPER LEFT quadrant represents their self-concept, how they feel about themselves when no one is looking.
My *intuitive* feelings about my partner are:

LOWER LEFT quadrant represents how they feel and express themselves in intimate relationships, and what they told themselves they were like in response to family dynamics.
My *intuitive* feelings about my partner are:

Summary Statements: Overall feelings about the two faces:

Myself:

My Partner:

Areas of Compatibility:

Areas that need strengthening or understanding between us:

Part II
Facial Features and What They Mean

The face, understood through the wisdom of physiognomy (Face Reading), is a record of inner emotions and life events. The hundreds of facial muscles form and change to reflect the state of a person's nervous system, their health, personality, disappointments and successes. By understanding others objectively, we can get along better with our families, our friends, and our business associates. In work, we can offer better service to our clients and interact more easily and effectively with bosses. Having a tangible skill for understanding people better, the student of Face Reading moves forward into healthier relationships.

For every physical facial feature, there is a list of corresponding psychological adjectives to describe someone who has that feature. Some of these descriptions will be positive; some will appear negative. There is always a *range* of temperament for each facial feature. A person with a certain feature may *not* have all the emotional characteristics listed of course, but will certainly have some. The key to learning Face Reading is to *ask* the person whose face you are reading *which* of the psychological descriptions of the features best describes them.

Note: The more pronounced a facial feature, the more intense it will be reflected in the persons's character. (**To form an overall picture of the person, facial features must be combined— See Part III)

THE THREE SECTIONS OF THE FACE AND WHAT THEY REVEAL

The face can be divided into three sections:

    The Ideas Section — the forehead to the eyebrow

    The Heart and Feeling Section — the eyebrows to the mouth

    The Will Section — the chin and jaw

IDEA SECTION

HEART AND FEELING

WILL SECTION

THE IDEAS SECTION: THE FOREHEAD

The area from the hairline to the eyebrows (the forehead) reveals a person's thinking style. Often when women cover this area with bangs, it indicates the possibility that they are integrating their emotional and will power areas (the two areas which are left visible), and are less interested in academic studies or financial matters at that time.

Mary, one of my clients, lowered her head to her hands as she sobbed out that her husband was dying of cancer. "It is so overwhelming taking care of Harry that I don't have energy left over to sort out all the financial aspects that go along with his hospital bills and our mortgage payments." I looked up sympathetically. Her thick, wavy hair was disheveled and cascaded down her high forehead.

Months after Harry had passed on, Mary stopped by to see me on her way back from the mortgage broker's office. She seemed much more confident and calmer, feeling happy about what she had negotiated with the bank. I noted her hair was pulled back away from her forehead, a hair band holding it securely. She had instinctually pulled her hair back to reveal her large, wide forehead. This facial feature projected: "I am intelligent. I have a forceful intention. Negotiate with me."

THE HEART AND FEELING SECTION:
THE CHEEKS

Extending from the eye area down through the cheeks, one sees by the shape, width, and length of the cheeks, to what extent emotions are expressed in the person's life. In the case of the actress Linda Evans, the cheeks, rounded and relaxed, show a vulnerable, open, loving person, one who might, under pressure, be too passive. A photo of J. Robert Oppenheimer, the "Father of the Atomic Bomb," shows, on the other hand, a cheek area that is very flat. This indicates a man whose natural focus was intellectual and theoretical.

THE WILL SECTION:
THE JAW AND CHIN

The shape, length and width of the jaw indicate quite a lot about the degree of stamina, assertiveness, and drive in a person's life.

Factors that indicate a forceful personality include:

- a wide or square jaw
- a forward-thrusting chin
- a long and wide jaw area
- a visually predominant lower section of the face.

Factors that indicate a shy or gentler soul include:

- a tapered (narrow) jaw
- a chin that recedes or is not predominant

READ WHAT YOU SEE

People naturally respond to us, consciously or unconsciously, by getting clues about us from our faces. They then make judgments and behave towards us based on what they see and feel. The ability to read others accurately and quickly is an innate survival instinct for the entire animal kingdom. Moreover, animals have naturally evolved in physical forms with features which help them hunt for food and survive. As humans we know whether an animal is dangerous or docile based on their physical features. When we see a hawk's talons, for example, we know this is an animal which flies high in the heavens and picks up small rodents on the ground. A kitten, on the other hand, is docile and affectionate. Over our lifetimes, our mental, emotional, and spiritual tendencies are recorded in our facial features, creating a distinct personality. Since no two of us have identical life experiences, no two of us look exactly alike.

Features with which we are born

These would include features such as close or wide-set eyes, a receding or forward thrusting jawline, high cheek bones. These features usually do not change.

What about ethnic traits? How do they fit in? There is an Italian restaurant in my neighborhood which is owned by a family with three beautiful daughters. Because I eat there so frequently, they had me read their faces. Even though they are all from the same ethnic background, and the same family, the girls' facial features and their personalities are very different. As you'll read in Part V, though Sara and Rachael are sisters, their facial features are very unique, and reflect their specific gifts and life lessons.

The goal of Face Reading is to understand our gifts and individuality as souls. For this reason, I ignore what might be interpreted as ethnic features, and look for what is *uniquely* personal for that individual. To assume facial features or personality traits will be universal for all people with the same ethnic background is not only false, but it is offensive. Such thinking goes completely against my own philosophy of Face Reading. Used in that context, Face Reading becomes a weapon, instead of a tool for personal inner growth and transformation, as it was intended.

Features that form in response to our emotions and thoughts

The soft tissue of our faces forms and changes in response to how we hold our mouths, or eyes, or jaws, for example, day after day. One who unconsciously frowns, for instance, because he or she is sad pulls the mouth muscles down, and over a period of time, downward diagonal lines begin to show around the mouth even when the person is at rest.

On the other hand, "crow's feet" around the eyes indicate a person who loves to smile, and who generally has a happy disposition. The only way to get these lines is by creasing the eye area in a smile. People often ask, "When we get older, doesn't everyone have 'crow's feet' or 'thin lips'?" As you look around you in the next few days, pay special attention to seniors and see if this theory is true. My observations suggest that it is how we live our lives, not our chronological age, that determines the facial features we have in later years. Abraham Lincoln, it is told, once refused to hire a man for a high level position in his cabinet because the man's face showed him to be dishonest.

How we can modify our original features to achieve the look we like

Examples of this are perming straight hair, growing a mustache or beard, applying eye makeup to make close-set eyes appear wider-set.

Clark Gable grew a pencil thin mustache, a feature attributed to a men who may be womanizers and yet fear intimacy. This was indeed Gable's public image before his loving marriage to Carole Lombard. In another example, Adolf Hitler felt comfortable with a "patch" mustache, a facial feature indicating paranoia and rage. Cher's long eyebrows, which extend from the inner eye orbit and circle her eye completely, correspond in Face Reading to a person who is wealthy, an actor or actress, and divorced.

Plastic surgery and accidents

Sometimes injuries and traumas occur that alter the face. How do we interpret these?

When a person has done inner emotional and mental healing work to prepare for the outer change in the muscles and tissues following a surgery, then the facial muscles support the surgery. It then looks natural. For example, Carol Burnett worked with her daughter in the latter's drug and alcohol recovery. Carol transformed herself in the process, becoming more dynamic. When Carol surgically had her receding chin brought forward (increasing her will power area or personal power area), it looked good.

Accidents can express sudden and drastic changes in the face. The key in interpreting trauma is to see if the psychological interpretation of the changed facial feature is expressed anywhere else in the face. If an emotion or tendency is very strong in a person's character, it will be recorded in several areas of the face. (ie: Goebbels of the Third Reich had a left cheek scar and he also had vacant eye tone, unusual ears, flat cheeks, and white under his eyes—features which when put together describe cruel attributes.) If, on the other hand, the trauma from an accident is not reflected on any other part of the face then give it minimal significance.

THE COMPLETE FACE:
PSYCHOLOGICAL MEANINGS OF THE FACIAL AREAS

HAIR reveals:
- degree of seriousness, sensitivity, and health of the body

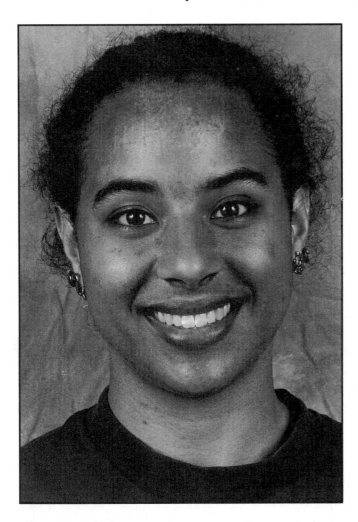

PHILTRUM (area from nostrils to upper lip) reveals:
- degree of sexual intensity
- constitutional or physical strength

JAW reveals:
- degree of willpower
- how one meets the world
- inner drive to succeed

EYEBROWS reveal:
- degree of personal power, aggressive or gentle nature

FOREHEAD reveals:
- thinking style
- degree of mental intensity

EYES reveal:
- spiritual wisdom
- one's "view" on things

EARS reveal:
- emotional and neurological tendencies
- how one tunes into the Big picture

CHEEKS reveal:
- how much feelings will be expressed

NOSE reveals:
- degree of financial or spiritual wealth

LIPS reveal:
- one's style of giving and receiving love and affection
- how one is in intimate relationships
- Upper lip: giving
- Lower lip: receiving

TEETH reveal:
- degree of personal power

CHIN reveals:
- how one moves forward in the world

Hair

<u>Straight hair</u>
serious minded, straight forward

<u>Curly hair</u>
lively, good sense of humor

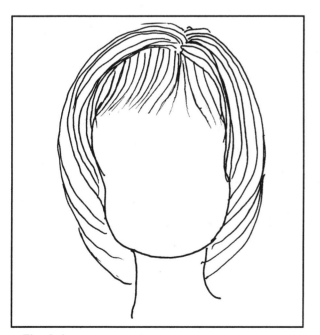

<u>Fine hair</u>
sensitive, gentle, the nervous or digestive
system can be easily upset

<u>Thick hair</u>
enjoys the outdoors, rugged, under pressure
may be abrupt

Hair Color

Blonde hair
fun loving,
sunny disposition,
self-confident

Red hair
fiery, intense,
dynamic

Brown hair
family (or support
system) oriented,
serious minded

Black hair
dominant or intense,
strong willed

Guidelines: When looking at hair color and evaluating its meaning, keep in mind that texture (fine or coarse) and whether the hair is straight, wavy or curly will also enter into the psychological assesment. For example, someone with black hair which is curly and fine will probably be more sensitive and lighthearted than someone with thick, straight black hair who would love hiking and the great outdoors.

Also (as covered in Part I), certain ethnic backgrounds may have a hair color (not necessarily the same texture of wave) which is predominant for them. For example, many people in Scandinavia are blonde, or those of Mediterranean origin have brown hair. How do you integrate this into your assessment? If you see traits which you think are more "ethnic" than uniquely personal, for that individual, ignore the "ethnic" traits. Then, look throughout the other areas of the face (forehead, lips, cheeks, ear height, etc.) to form an accurate and *personal* interpretation of the soul before you. In Face Reading, you are looking for that which makes the person before you *special* in gifts and hidden potentials.

Forehead

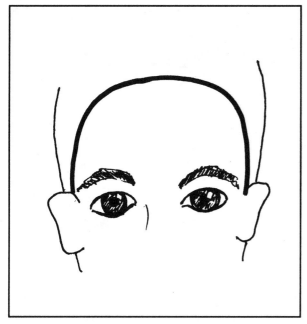

Rounded forehead
makes friends easily, long-term friendships, peaceful and spiritual

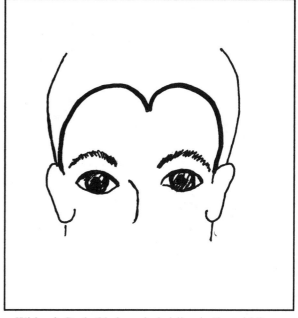

Widow's Peak (V-shape in hairline in the middle of forehead)
likes a relaxed lifestyle, (sweats and blue jeans), artistic and creative

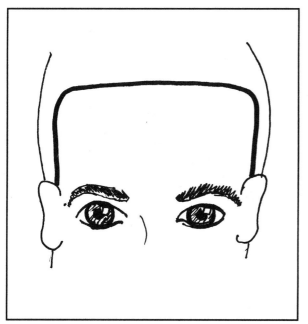

Square forehead
career-oriented, works long hours, (can be a workaholic)

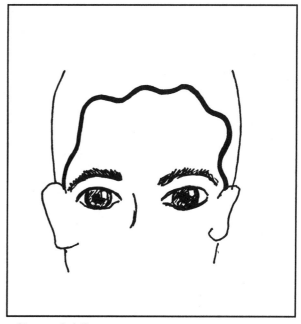

Uneven hairline
childhood may have been chaotic or non-nurturing

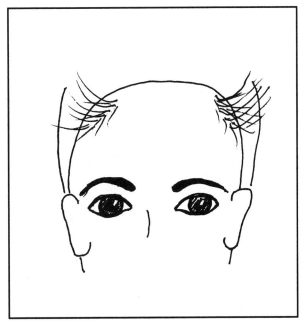

<u>Wispy outer corners of hairline</u>
their mother had a significant impact in their
personal (Left) or professional life (Right)

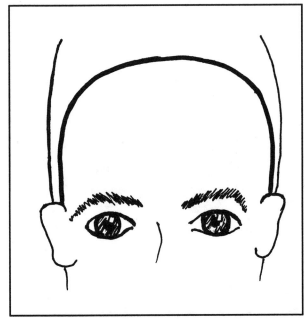

<u>Large, wide forehead (forehead long and high)</u>
thinks in "big" terms, clear thinker, intelligent

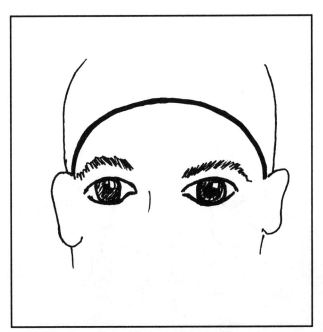

<u>Short forehead (height from eyebrows)</u>
intuitive, trusts their "gut" responses to situations,
"street smart"

Forehead Lines

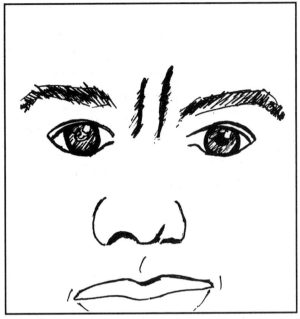

Two vertical lines (parallel) above nose
focused, under pressure may worry
or be compulsive

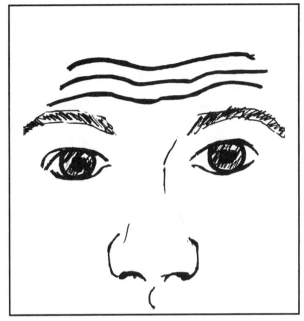

Three (parallel) horizontal lines above the nose
good fortune and wealth

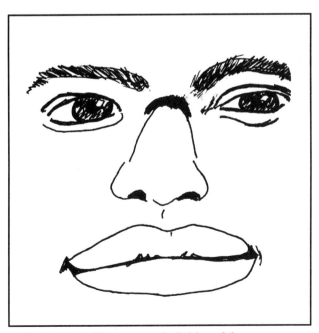

One horizontal line across the bridge of the nose
expert in their area <u>or</u> may be intensely angry

27

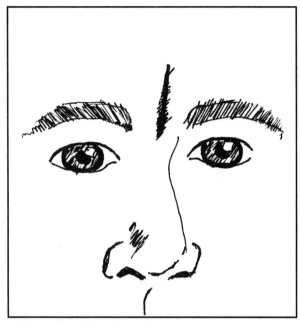

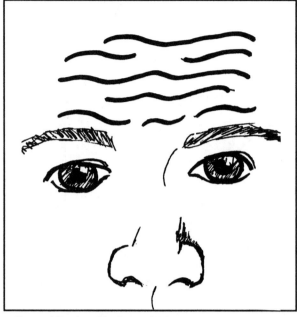

<u>One vertical line above the nose</u>
self-made person, goes in completely different
direction (spiritually, emotionally or professionally)
than family-of-origin

<u>Several Broken Horizontal Lines</u>
may have 55 mental projects going at the same time,
under stress their ideas may get scattered

Eye Color

Hazel eye color
takes on 20 projects at once!
easily bored, mentally agile,
under pressure may be restless

Green eye color
curious, intelligent, under stress
may be jealous

Brown eye color
cares deeply for family,
or support system, affectionate,
serious nature

Light blue eye color
peaceful, may have low
physical endurance

Dark blue eye color
spiritual, intense, left-brained
(may love computers!)

Blue-grey eye color
benefit focused, humanitarian,
may wish to remain anonymous
in doing good deeds

Grey eye color
analytical, clear thinking,
philosophical (if "steel" grey,
may be calculating or have
shrewd judgement)

Eyes

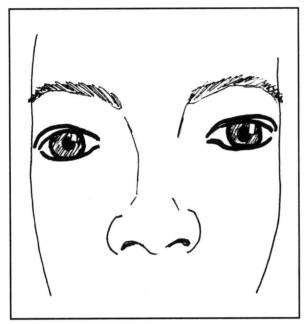

Wide-set eyes (the distance between the two eyes is greater than one eye's length)
sees the "whole" picture, kind-hearted, may procrastinate or show up late for appointments

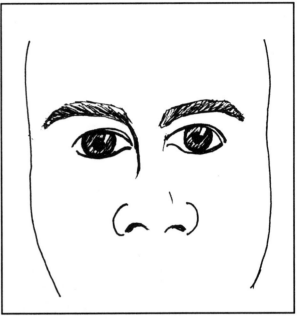

Close-set eyes (the distance between the two eyes is less than one eye's length)
precision-oriented, does well with details, under pressure may be a perfectionist

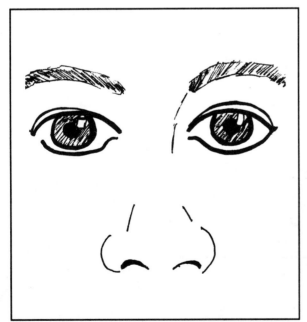

Large eye size (eyes appear large for their face size)
sentimental, soft hearted, generous, may not notice if others take advantage of them

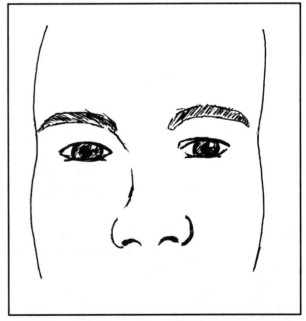

Small eye size (eyes appear small for their face size)
Sees everything around them! Doesn't miss a detail!

Area Around the Eyes

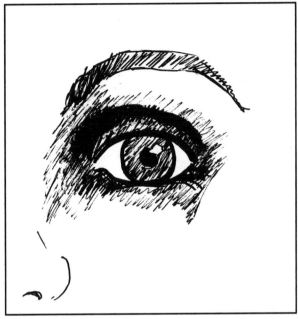

<u>In-set eyes</u>
deep thinker, philosophical, may be introvert

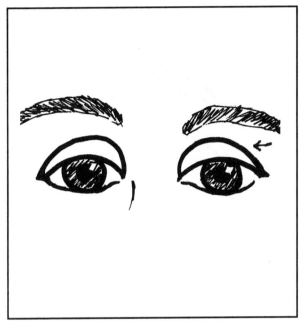

<u>Visible eyelids (eyelids show above eyes)</u>
action-oriented doer, likes to get things done <u>now</u>!

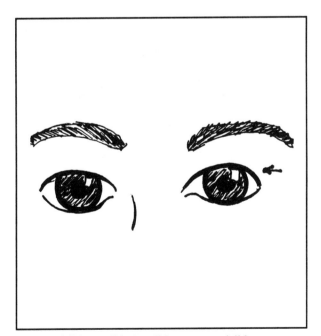

<u>Non-visible eyelids (eyelids are not visible
above the eyes)</u>
planner of projects, likes to set up systems,
list maker

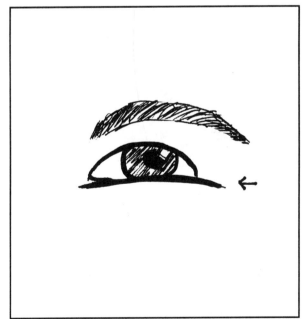

<u>Flat lower eyelid</u>
cautious, wary, "waits to see" with people

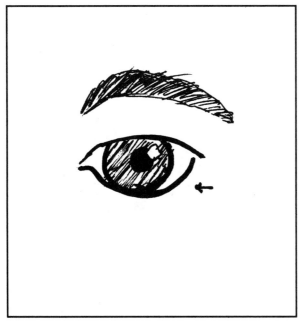

<u>Rounded lower eyelid</u>
sentimental, keeps scrapbooks from high school prom, romantic

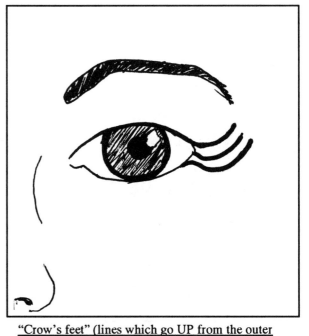

<u>"Crow's feet" (lines which go UP from the outer edge of the eye)</u>
sense of humor, sunny disposition, enjoys witty people

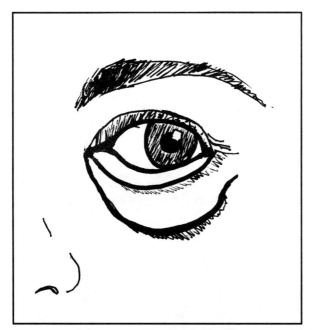

<u>Grief bags (watery looking bags under the eyes)</u>
unresolved grieving, holding back the tears

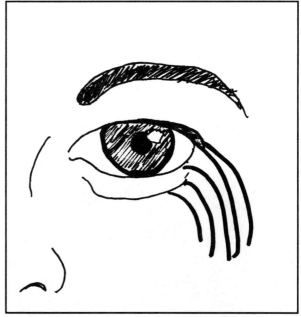

<u>"Teacher lines" (lines going DOWN from the outer corner of the eye — going across the cheek)</u>
gifted with the written word, teaching or oral communication, aware of grammar, with inner wisdom, sometimes "laughs to avoid crying"

Eyebrows: Size and Shape

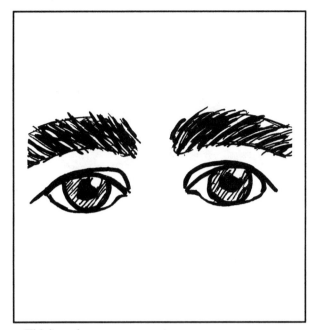

Thick eyebrows
abrupt, dominant, or intense

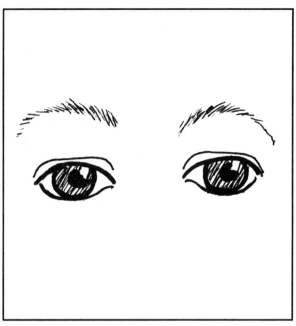

Thin eyebrows (pencil like)
very sensitive, may be high-strung under
pressure, may have low physical endurance

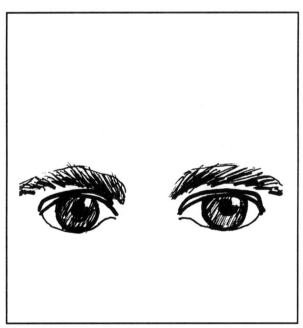

Low-set eyebrows (distance between eyes and
eyebrows is small)
friendly, easily approachable, under stress may be
overly familiar

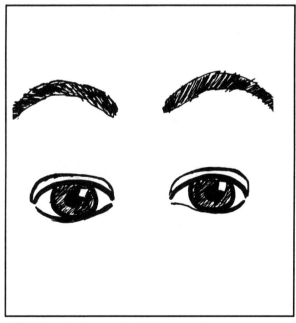

High (eyebrows are high above eyes)
high standards, not easily impressed by others, hand
select their friends and are loyal to them

Eyebrow Shapes
(continued)

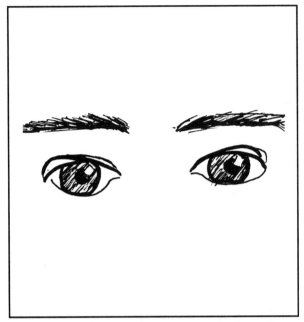

Flat eyebrows (appear straight across, horizontal)
shy or introverted or artistic

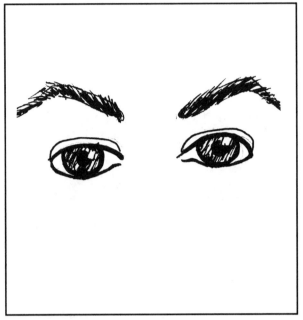

Arched eyebrows
powerful, dynamic, under stress may have an
angry disposition

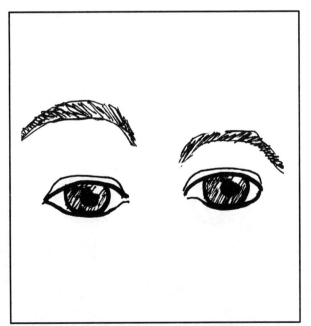

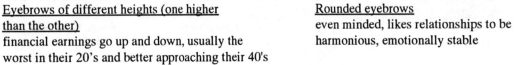

Eyebrows of different heights (one higher
than the other)
financial earnings go up and down, usually the
worst in their 20's and better approaching their 40's

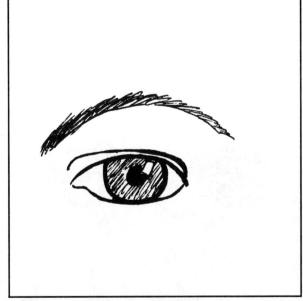

Rounded eyebrows
even minded, likes relationships to be
harmonious, emotionally stable

Eyebrow Shapes
(continued)

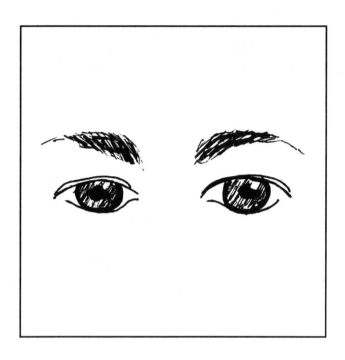

<u>Brows stop at the mid-point</u>
struggles hard with life and problems (needs
to discriminate those issues which require
intense energy and those which do not)

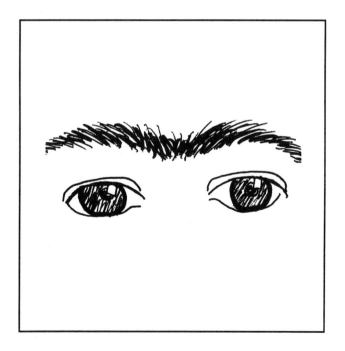

<u>Joined eyebrows (hairs growing into the
middle area above the nose)</u>
introverted, intense, under stress may be
cruel or aggressive

Cheek Contours

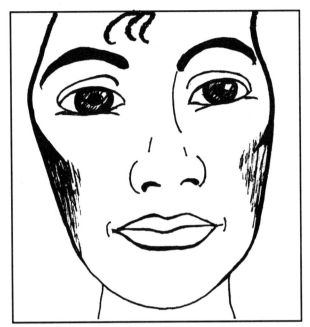

<u>High cheekbones (the bone is apparent)</u>
high-spirited, loves to travel, prefers to be
self-employed

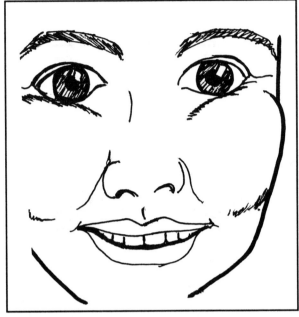

<u>Rounded cheeks (full)</u>
feeling-oriented, loving, under stress, may be
passive

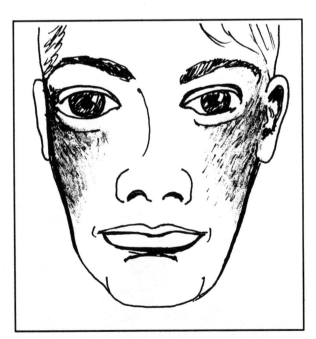

<u>Flat or hollow cheeks</u>
mental type—may intellectualize their
feelings instead of feeling them

<u>Left strong nasolabial line (line that goes diagonally
from nose to mouth)</u>
in early childhood were not allowed to express their
negative emotions (anger, fear, guilt) so are learning
these skills—negotiation and communication—now.

Noses

Large, (fleshy) nose
abundance: financial, spiritual, or both

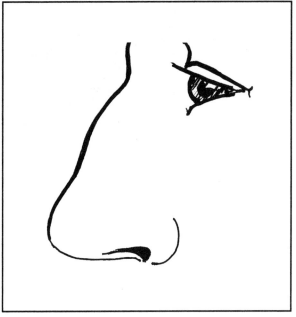

Nose bows OUT
handles money and investments well

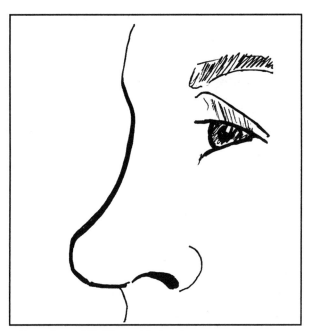

Nose bows IN (like a ski-slope)
enjoys caring for or giving service to others

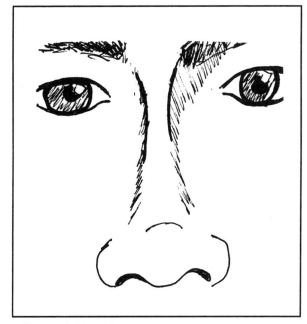

Narrow bridge of upper nose
loner, may enjoy classical music (strings), under
stress may be a perfectionist

<u>Hawk nose (end of nose points down and looks
like a beak)</u>
ambitious, under stress may be gossipy
or treacherous

<u>Nostrils are visible at eye level</u>
Money comes to them, and they spend freely.

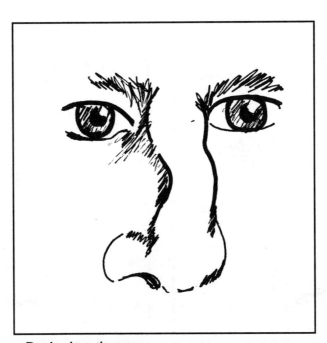

<u>Breaks along the nose</u>
traumas or major life changes at various ages:
*At bridge, near eyes—during teens
*1/3 down - mid to late 20's
*1/2 down - in 30's   *Nose tip - old age

Philtrum
(grooved area under nose and above upper lip)

Long philtrum (long distance between the lip and nose)
can take constructive criticism well

Short philtrum (short distance between the lip and nose)
needs self-validation and feedback, under stress may be overly influenced by flattery

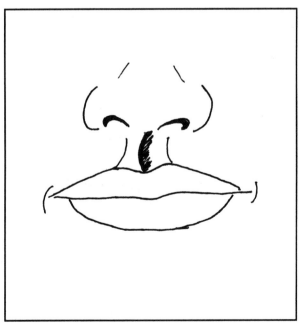

Well-defined or flared philtrum (strong line)
strong, sexual energy, good physical endurance

Flat or no philtrum
may have low energy, tires easily, needs to learn to draw on inner energy in midlife (yoga, tai chi, karate, meditation, etc.)

Mouth and Lip Shapes

<u>Small mouth (mouth size the same as nose width)</u>
rich fantasy life, under stress may be critical,
self-absorbed or dangerous to cross swords with

<u>Wide mouth (width, not lip shape)</u>
affectionate, generous, under stress may be nervous
about being abandoned in intimate relationships

<u>Full lips (shape of upper and lower lips)</u>
generous, sensual, passionate

<u>Thin lips (lips barely visible)</u>
business oriented and efficient, may be
cool emotionally

Mouth and Lip Shapes
(continued)

Lines turned down at the corners of the mouth
sadness or depression, may have had many
emotional losses

Protruding lower lip (lower lip larger and
thicker than upper lip—comes forward)
sensual, sassy, or pouting

Balanced lips (upper and lower are equal in size)
want to give and receive equally in an intimate
relationship, emotionally balanced

Large upper lip
giver, loves to take care of others, under stress may
want to control their gifts (to see <u>where</u> their
donations go!)

Large Lower Lip (with thin upper lip)
private person, can keep confidences,
under stress may be a taker

"Self-esteem" marks (appear like dimples or
indentations on the right or left side of the mouth)
Right: may have had to search through many
occupations before they are happy in a profession.

"Self-esteem" mark on the Left:
on an emotional level they are learning to
"re-parent" their negative self-talk into positive
mental affirmations

Teeth

<u>Space between two front teeth</u>
loss in early childhood: divorce of parents, poverty
and/or abandonment issues

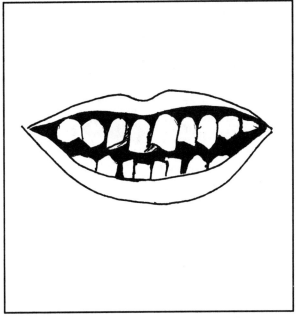

<u>Chaotic teeth (go in different directions or have
spaces in between them)</u>
may have had emotionally chaotic childhood

<u>Large front teeth</u>
dislikes being controlled (determined), under
stress may be stubborn

Teeth
(continued)

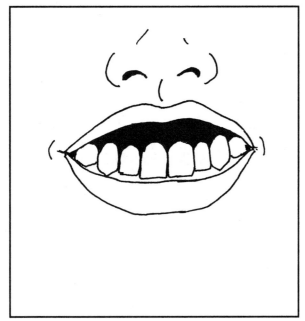

<u>Visible gum line (gums show above teeth when smiling)</u>
finances are a life challenge! they budget-budget, and then they spend!

<u>Small, even teeth</u>
quick learner, may shy away from positions of power

Ears

Ear Height: To determine the height of the ears as related to the eyes put your hand on the top of your ear and trace a straight line from the top of the ear, across the face, to the eyes. Note if the ears are level, or below or above the eye level.

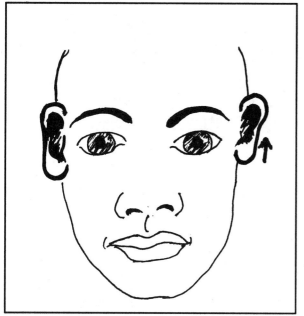

Hyphen-placed ears (top of ear lies above the eye level)

High-placed ears (top of ear lies above
the eye level)
does well in academic situations, good memory

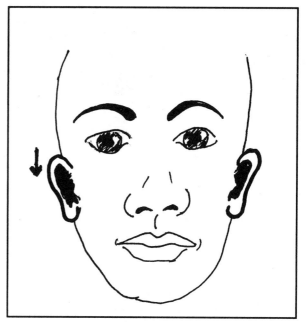

Low-placed ears (top of ear lies below eye level)
late-bloomers in life, success comes usually
between the 30's and 40's, intuitive

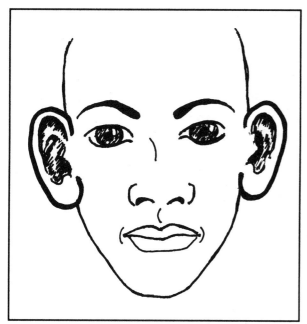

Ears protrude from head
musical ability, (right ear: music as profession; left
ear: music as hobby), independent or non-conformist

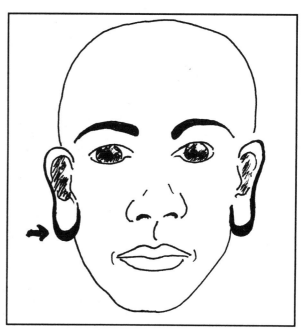

Long lobes (Buddha had lobes to his shoulders)
inner wisdom and spiritual understanding

Ears (continued)

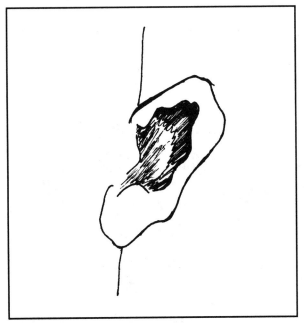

<u>Very unusual ears (come out from the head at an angle)</u>
may reflect emotional or neurological imbalances (at worst—criminal tendencies)

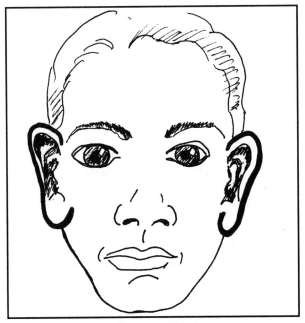

<u>Large ears (for size of the rest of the head)</u>
good listener, tunes in to the "big" picture

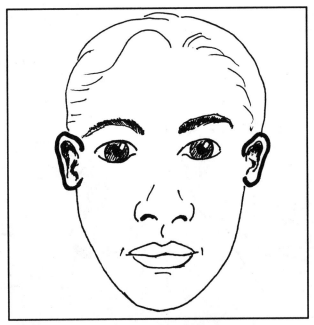

<u>Small ears (for size of the rest of the head)</u>
may hear "qpf" when someone says "abc", under stress may be self-absorbed or dishonest

Ears (continued)

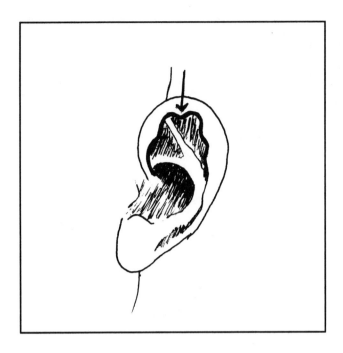

Inner-ear rim at top is curvy
may have been bored in early
schooling, or academics did not
meet their emotional or
intellectual needs

Inner-ear middle protrudes
New Age interests (tai chi, yoga,
macrobiotics, meditation, creative thinking)

Chins

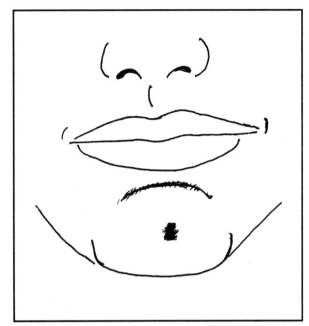

Dimpled chin
strong desire to be loved, may have
strong sex drive

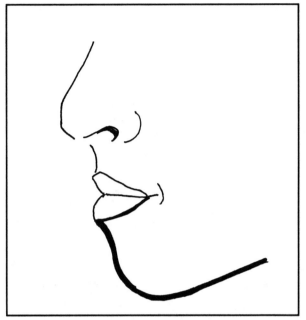

Receding chin
gentle, likes to avoid conflict, under
stress may be too passive

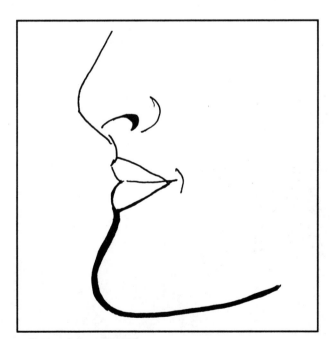

Forward thrusting chin
go-getter, makes lemonade out of
lemons! under stress may be aggressive

Chins (continued)

Rounded chin
tender, kind-hearted, sweet

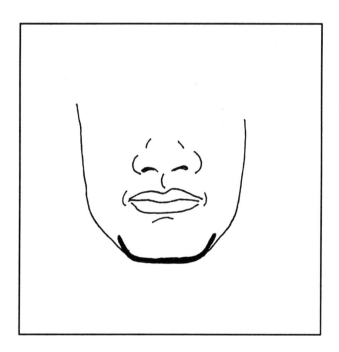

Square chin
builder, likes things to advance
steadily (financially, physically,
emotionally—on all levels)

Jaw Shapes

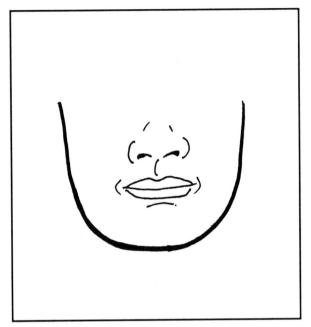

Broad jaw
dominant, strong will-power, under
stress may be without compassion

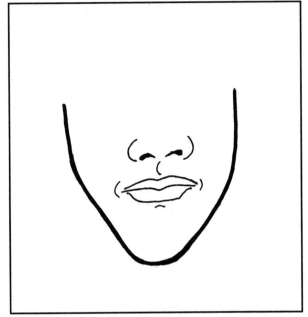

Tapered jaw
gentle, gifted but shy, will need to learn
assertiveness and how to set emotional boundaries

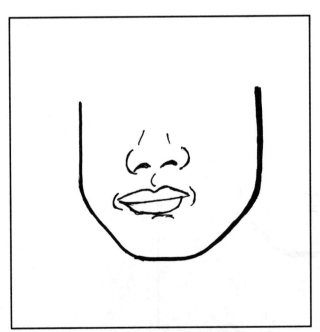

Left side of jaw is wider than the right side
emotionally harder on themselves than they are on
other people

PART II: EXERCISES WITH PARTNER

(1)   In this approach you will *list* the first four or five *outstanding facial features* you notice when looking at your partner.

(2)   After having read Part II of this book, list the character adjectives which describe these facial features.

(3)   Ask your partner which of the many adjectives listed describes them best.

(4)   Underline or check adjectives or major themes that repeat (ie: intelligent, artistic, extrovert, etc.)

Four or five things I notice about my partner	Adjectives that go with these features
(Ex: low eyebrows)	(Ex: friendly, easy to know, you are at once at home with them, etc.)
1)	1)
2)	2)
3)	3)
4)	4)
5)	5)

PART II: EXERCISES WITH PARTNER

(1)   In this approach you will *list* the first four or five *outstanding facial features* you notice when looking at your partner.

(2)   After having read Part II of this book, list the character adjectives which describe these facial features.

(3)   Ask your partner which of the many adjectives listed describes them best.

(4)   Underline or check adjectives or major themes that repeat (ie: intelligent, artistic, extrovert, etc.)

Four or five things I notice about my partner	Adjectives that go with these features
(Ex: low eyebrows)	(Ex: friendly, easy to know, you are at once at home with them, etc.)
1)	1)
2)	2)
3)	3)
4)	4)
5)	5)

PUTTING IT ALL TOGETHER
THE WORKSHEET FOR COMPATIBILITY

In the following chart, compare *you and your partner* to see how compatible you are:

Name:_____

Partner's Name:_____

Facial Features	We are the *same* (✓)	We are *different* (✓)
1) **Three AREAS of the face** Which is the *biggest* area of your face? Of your partner's face?		
Forehead (intellectual)		
Cheeks (emotional)		
Jaw (will)		
2) **HAIR**		
Color (brown, blonde, etc.)		
Texture (fine, coarse)		
Type (curly, straight, wavy)		

Facial Features	We are the *same* (✔)	We are *different* (✔)
3) UPPER FOREHEAD (thinking style)		
Square or rounded		
Large/wide, or narrow/short		
Widow's peak, other features		
Forehead lines (how many? where?)		
4) EYES		
color (dark/light blue, green, grey, etc.)		
close-set or wide-set		
large or small		
eyelids (visible, non-visible)		
eyebrows (thick, thin)		
shape (flat, angled, rounded)		
5) CHEEK SHAPE		
High cheekbones; flat or rounded cheeks		
6) NOSE		
large or small		
nostrils (visible, non-visible)		
breaks in the nose		

Facial Features	We are the *same* (✓)	We are *different* (✓)
7) PHILTRUM (area under nose and above the upper lip)		
long or short		
grooved or flat		
8) MOUTH and LIPS		
width		
lip shape (full, thin; upper lip larger, lower lip larger)		
9) TEETH		
size		
front teeth		
visible gums above teeth		
TOTALS		

Part III

The <u>Whole</u> Face...

Combining
Facial Features

In Face Reading as in mathematics, a beginner starts by learning basic concepts. In math, the concept "4" might refer to four apples lined up in a row. "Six" oranges means one can count out six sweet orange fruits. So far, we have looked at each <u>individual</u> facial feature and its corresponding personality or character attribute. Now, we will start combining them, or adding them together, to form a more intricate picture or understanding.

In the following cartoon examples, I have taken the drawings from Part II and reduced them in size. As you look at them, see if there are personality traits that <u>repeat</u> or are somewhat similar (ie: friendly, out-going, warm hearted, etc.) The more of these there are which are similar, the stronger that mental and emotional tendency will be in the person's character. None of us have faces which are 100% "outgoing" or "shy." There is usually a combination of tendencies. When analyzing a combination of tendencies, mentally imagine a scale with equal weights on it to start. If four of the facial features suggest an "extrovert," "warm hearted," "easy to get to know," and "has many friends" and only one facial feature suggests "a loner type" of person, then your imaginary scale tips towards the outgoing quality. The person is probably predominately outgoing and a people person. If, on the other hand, two of the tendencies are "warm hearted," and "has many friends" and two of the other facial features suggest "a loner," and "shy," then this person is more of an introvert than the first example.

KEY: In the next Section of Questions, look at the first feature and think about its meaning (refer to Part II, Drawings, if you need to). Then, look at the next feature and reflect on what a person would be like if they had these two together. Now, put the third one with the other two to get a fuller picture of the individual. Then think, what this person would be like as a boss? An employee? A friend? A girlfriend/boyfriend/spouse? Would you like them? Could you trust them? What are their strengths and weaknesses?

DATING IN THE 90'S

WHERE WOULD YOU EXPECT TO FIND *THIS* PERSON AT A *PARTY?*

a) in the corner under the fern reading a book

b) on the table in the middle of the room, telling jokes to the group

c) in the kitchen discussing German philosophers with a girlfriend

Character analysis: This affectionate and friendly (wide mouth) person is very people oriented (lower lid) and fun loving (curly hair). They will enjoy large parties and probably be the center of attention.

_____

   Answer: (b)

IN WHICH <u>OCCUPATION</u> WILL THIS PERSON FEEL <u>MOST</u> AT HOME?

a) airplane pilot

b) third grade school teacher

c) structural engineer

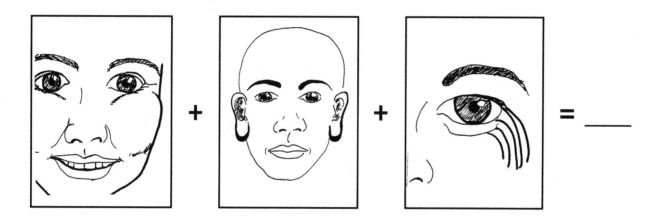

Character Analysis: The "teacher lines" and the full cheeks combined would suggest someone who would enjoy sharing ideas or skills with children. The long lobes add to this an innate wisdom and understanding to impart. This person might also be a writer of insightful and engaging novels.

Answer: (b)

FRIENDS: ON TIME?

*YOUR NEW FRIEND IS MEETING YOU FOR TEA. FROM HIS OR HER FACE,
YOU WOULD EXPECT THEM TO BE:*

a) on time!

b) at least 25 minutes late.

c) a "no show". (They lied when they said they'd meet you!)

Character Analysis: This conscientious person (straight hair) values people and their friends (low-set eyebrows). To have attained this level of wealth and power (three horizontal lines above the eyes), this is a person who learned to keep the agreements they make to others.

Answer: (a)

SHOPPING

THIS PERSON LOVES TO "SHOP TILL THEY DROP" AT:

a) the local dime store

b) the most expensive clothier in the city

c) toy stores

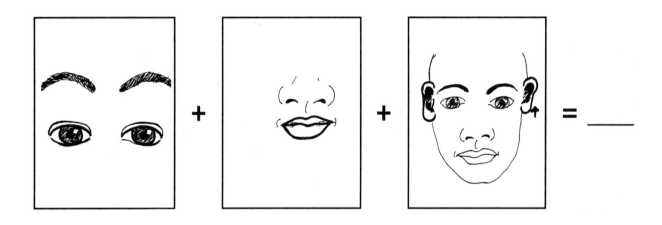

Character Analysis: The refinement (high eyebrows) and the high ears suggest an intelligent person who is looking for value in things. The small mouth adds the quality of critically evaluating purchases. This person would probably make a good buyer for a prestigious art gallery!

Answer (b)

MARRIAGE

WHAT WILL BE THE <u>HARDEST AREA OF ADJUSTMENT</u> FOR THIS PERSON IN AN INTIMATE RELATIONSHIP?

a) career choices and work

b) sex and physical closeness

c) budgeting and money issues

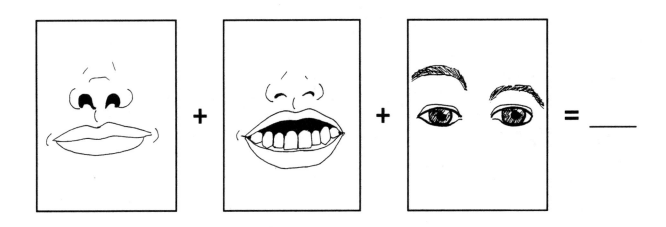

Character Analysis: Each of these three features expresses an easy, open style with spending money—especially the first and third. "The money comes in; the money goes out!"

Answer: (c)

JOB CHANGES?

WHICH <u>CAREER</u> SUITS THIS PERSON?

a) a car mechanic who loves working with machinery

b) a public relations specialist

c) a forest ranger who sits in a tower watching for summer fires

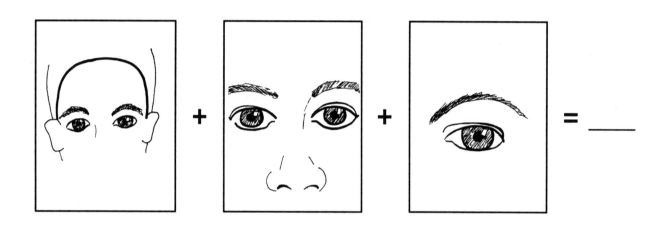

Character analysis: A people-person from the start, this person has a gift for tact and friendship (rounded hairline), is generous (large eyes) and balanced (even eyebrows.) They will be able to handle difficult people and challenging people-problems with warmth and sincerity.

Answer: (b)

WHAT KIND OF BOSS IS THIS PERSON?
WHAT WILL THEY WANT OF YOU?

a) an entrepeuner, workaholic: Their motto: " Work till you drop."

b) relaxed, flexible: Their motto: "Tomorrow is another day!"

c) soft spoken and gentle: Their motto: "Be seen and not heard."

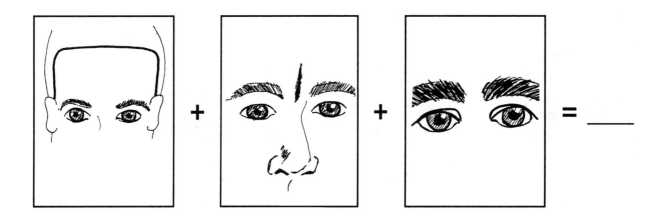

Character analysis: This person is a self-starter, (one vertical line between eyes), career oriented go-getter (square hairline) with intensity (eyebrows)! They will probably own their own company and expect you to put in the hours they put in!

_____

Answer: (a)

MOTHER-IN-LAW?

YOUR SON INTRODUCES YOU TO HIS DATE WHO HAS THESE FEATURES. WHAT CAN YOU SEE ABOUT <u>HER FAMILY</u> BACKGROUND?

a) many siblings present but nurturing parents

b) born with a "silver spoon" - wealthy, powerful and loving family

c) Was it rough! chaotic or not personally nurturing for this person.

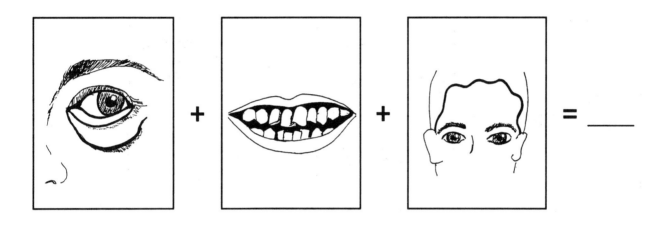

Character analysis: The sadness in the eyes (grief bags) and the uneven hairline and teeth suggest emotional turmoil in childhood in the family-of-origin. (However, if love, nurturing and guidance came from outside people (perhaps teachers, counselors, ministers, relatives, etc.), this person may have turned their "lemons" into "lemonade" and have dynamic "recovery"—compassion, wisdom and inner strength.)

Answer: (c)

WOULD YOU <u>HIRE</u> THIS PERSON?

*YOU OWN YOUR OWN BUSINESS AND NEED ONE MORE EMPLOYEE
FOR <u>PERSONNEL AND PUBLIC RELATIONS.</u> WILL THIS PERSON
BE HAPPY AND DO WELL? ON THE JOB THEY WILL PROBABLY BE:*

a) calm and easy-going

b) honest and efficient

c) angry or deceitful

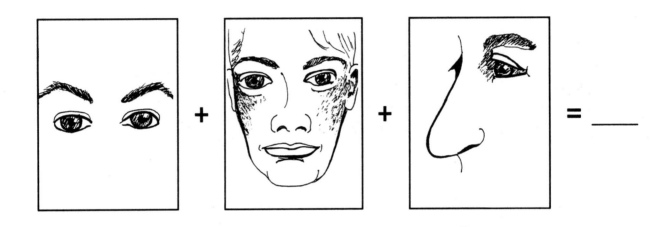

Character analysis: A powerful or at times explosive (eyebrows) personality, the cheeks and nose suggest someone better suited to mental or mechanical work than work involving people's feelings and potentially delicate verbal negotiations.

Answer: (c)

Part IV
Individual Face Readings

KAYOKO

MAJOR FEATURES:

- short-rounded forehead
- fine hair
- high-placed eyebrows (flat across)
- nostrils visible from the front
- high cheekbones
- balanced lips
- self-esteem marks on right and left sides of the mouth
- long ear lobes
- large front teeth
- large jaw (L>R)
- chin forward and round

CHARACTER ANALYSIS:

Independence is a big factor for Kayoko (large front teeth, high cheekbones, chin forward), and yet she is sensitive to the needs of her friends and family (rounded forehead and fine hair). An intelligent (high ears) person, she has good intuition and relies a lot on her inner guidance (long ear lobes, short rounded hairline). Though somewhat shy by nature (high eyebrows and L self-esteem mark on the mouth, jaw larger L>R), she is nonetheless very loving (rounded chin and balanced lips) when she is comfortable in the relationship. She has a genuine kindness and sensitive awareness (fine hair, rounded chin, balanced lips).

LIFE CHALLENGE(S) AND GROWTH:

Finances and career (R self-esteem mark on mouth, low ears, visible nostrils) have been a challenge for her. When in times of stress, she experiences aspects of self-doubt (L jaw>R jaw) or self-criticism, she leans more to her natural spiritual intuition. Her high cheekbones with large front teeth and fine hair shaft suggest someone who would prefer to be self-employed, using their artistic creativity.

MEKAYLA

MAJOR FEATURES:

- high & broad forehead
- wispy hair on corners of forehead
- fine, blonde hair
- brown eyes
- lower eyelids are straight across
- low-set eyebrows
- right eyebrow rounded
- left eyebrow arched
- high placed ears, which come forward
- large cheeks
- left nasolabial line stronger than right
- large jaw structure
- thin upper lip
- gums show above teeth

CHARACTER ANALYSIS:

Mekayla is a complex combination of high intellectual ability (high, broad forehead and high ears) with a strongly determined will (large jaw). She will be both sensitive (large cheeks and fine hair shaft) and family oriented (wispy hair on corners of forehead, deep brown eyes, full cheeks, low-set eyebrows) and at the same time dynamic and willful. Her strong spirit has much kindness within.

LIFE CHALLENGE(S) AND GROWTH:

Her high energy must be guided without suppressing her will or she could become selfish (thin upper lip) or argumentative (strong nasolabial line on the left, left arched eyebrow). Mekayla may be naturally musical (ears come forward) or artistic. She will spend money freely (gums over the teeth) with an innate sense of elegance and value (fine, blonde hair).

THELMA

MAJOR FEATURES:

- short forehead
- curly, fine hair
- low-set eyebrows
- "teacher lines" at eyes
- "crow's feet" at eyes
- small eyes
- visible eyelids
- large nose
- full cheeks
- high-placed ears
- thin upper lip
- round chin

CHARACTER ANALYSIS:

Thelma is a generous (large nose, full cheeks, bright eye tone, rounded chin), down-to-earth person (small eyes, short forehead) with sensitivity to the needs of others (fine hair shaft, full cheeks). At a young age of 92 (!), Thelma has an enthusiastic or "giving" outlook on life (the nose) combined with a bright sense of optimism ("crow's feet").

The "teacher lines" at her eyes combined with the fine hair shaft and full cheeks reveal a sincere, deeply feeling person, who is articulate in sharing her feelings. The low eyebrows show her natural friendliness. At the same time the visible eyelids combined with the small eyes indicate a "let's do it now," a no-nonsense, action-oriented person who would not like to procrastinate.

AREAS OF CHALLENGE(S) OR GROWTH:

At 92, Thelma looks amazing! Whatever she is doing certainly works!

Part V

Relationships: What We Can Learn From Others

COMPATIBILITY

All life involves getting along with others. Face Reading offers a practical skill for understanding those around us and thereby getting along better with them. When we can look at people and see their inner needs and personalities, we can give them better service in business. We can see and maximize the gifts and hidden potentials in our children. By letting go of unrealistic expectations about others, our intimate relationships have room to heal and to grow.

The theory behind Face Reading is that our mental, emotional and spiritual tendencies have come down into the physical body to be delicately recorded in the facial features. Based on this assumption, **people who look the most like us (having similar facial features) will have mental, emotional, and spiritual tendencies in common with our own.** They may have our tendency to worry or procrastinate on deadlines, or they may have a similar style in spending money. Features that are similar reach across ethic, age, and differences of gender to make two people compatible in thought and spirit who come from completely different backgrounds or parts of the world. This is not to say that those with dissimilar faces cannot be our close friends or teach us valuable skills and lessons. We can learn from everyone if we are open.

In intimate relationships, which will be for a lifetime, happy, flowing connections? And which will always have an edge of tension and stress? In intimate relationships, such as marriage, I believe the **best compatibility for partners occurs when about 70%+ of their facial features are "complimentary."** When we look 100% like a spouse or boyfriend/girlfriend, over time boredom may set in. There may be no mystery or "spark!"

What does "complementary" mean in practical terms?

1) Facial features that are exactly the same:
   Both people have black hair. Both have visible eyelids. Foreheads for the two are high and broad.

2) The eye colors are either the same (deep blue to deep blue) or of similar intensity (light blue to light green; deep hazel to deep brown).

3) The shapes of the features are similar:
   Both have tapered jaws. The shape of the eyes and eyelids look the same. The cheeks on both people are full and rounded. Both have angular or delicate bone structures.

4) The textures of a feature are the same:
   Both people have fine hair or both have wavy hair. The eyebrows of the two are thick and bushy. Both have very thick hair.

WHEN OPPOSITES ATTRACT

The greater the number of dissimilar facial features (over about 30%—see the worksheets following Part II), the more innate tension will be in a relationship. As the initial chemistry or spontaneity of the relationship calms, our natural and comfortable range of behaviors (as expressed in our facial features) will come forward. We settle back into the way we "usually" are in our daily life and personal habits. Then we may not be as harmonious with our partner's natural and comfortable range of behaviors (as expressed by their facial features which are so different from our own.) Basic misunderstandings arise because the two people have different styles in facing finances, children, work, sex, etc. There is no right or wrong "face" nor facial feature. There is no right or wrong "style" in living life. The reason for using Face Reading in looking at long term compatibility is simply to assist us in choosing wisely when it comes to making important life-altering decisions such as marriage or choosing business partners.

When do opposites do well together?

Suppose I am very shy and you, my partner, mix easily with people. Conflict may arise if I resent your extroverted personality, am jealous of your out-going nature or seek to limit or control you. Both of us will then be miserable. You will feel trapped by my wanting to confine you, and I would feel abandoned or angry and too isolated. If, on the other hand, I enjoy your "style" or even want to learn from you how to broaden my own social skills, then neither of us feels trapped. Then we both benefit. By enjoying and accepting those parts of our partner's personalities which our own face or temperament does not express (assuming those qualities are not damaging), the relationship becomes more relaxed and fun!

SISTERS: SARA AND RACHAEL

MAJOR FEATURES (SARA):

- square hairline
- close-set eyes
- visible eyelids
- rounded eyebrows
- nasolabial lines curves around the mouth
- high ears, inner rims turn back on themselves
- teeth even and straight across
- powerful jaw
- rounded chin

CHARACTER ANALYSIS:

Sara is a builder and a hard worker (square hairline, close-set eyes, visible eyelids). She has a strong will (jaw) and likes to move on things and get things accomplished (powerful jaw, square hairline, close-set eyes). She is a quick learner (teeth even and straight across). Intelligent (high ears) and articulate (nasolabial lines curve around the mouth), her tenderness balances these other qualities (as expressed in her rounded chin and rounded eyebrows).

Interested in unusual or artistic projects (inner ear rims), she would enjoy the precision of calligraphy or graphic arts (close-set eyes, square hairline). She is also honest (the two sides of the face are the same). "What you see is what you get." She knows what she wants, is focused and goal oriented. Her eye tone also reflects a quiet or introspective spiritual nature.

AREAS OF LIFE CHALLENGE OR GROWTH:

Whenever so many features on the face show concentration and focus, the person may have a hard time being wild and crazy when they want to be spontaneous or frivolous. Under stress, Sara might become a perfectionist or be too hard on herself.

MAJOR FEATURES: (RACHAEL)

- rounded hairline
- wide-set eyes
- visible eyelids
- rounded eyebrows
- nasolabial lines curve around the mouth
- large front teeth
- lower ears than Sara's
- rounded chin

CHARACTER ANALYSIS:

Rachael is a people-person (rounded hairline, nasolabial lines curve around the mouth) who is interested in the feelings and well-being of others (rounded chin, wide-set eyes, rounded hairline). She is so generous and good hearted (wide-set eyes, rounded hairline, wide mouth) that animals and children love her. Of all the family members, my guess is she is the one who feeds the dog! If she is focused on her friends or animals, she may get frustrated (large front teeth) if she is unexpectedly rushed into then doing an activity that requires precision or motor skills. Naturally affectionate (rounded eyebrows, rounded chin, wide-set eyes, rounded hairline), she will probably choose a profession working with the public. However, she may be a late bloomer (low ears).

Rachael will be more of an extrovert (wide-set eyes and wide mouth with rounded chin) than her sister, Sara, having lots of friends and enjoying social contacts. She will be very verbal (nasolabial lines) and yet sensitive to other's feelings (rounded cheeks, and rounding at eyebrows and hairline).

LIFE CHALLENGE(S) OR GROWTH:

Rachael may need to allow herself more time to focus when projects are detailed or complex analytically. Probably a good creative writer and dancer, she might have to struggle more with areas of advanced math or the sciences. Because she is so open hearted, occasionally people will take advantage of her generosity, and this will be painful for her. Discrimination in who to tell what to and who to trust will be a skill she will develop as she gets older.

WHAT THEY CAN LEARN FROM EACH OTHER:

        Rachael can learn from Sara's mental concentration, precision, and goal orientation. Being a high achiever and somewhat introverted, Sara will need privacy and quiet time to concentrate and to develop her ideas and creativity. Sara might also feel in conflict or get frustrated if she has project deadlines and Rachael is at the same time emotionally upset by something and not easily soothed. Rachael on the other hand has a natural love of life and a generous free spirit which Sara will enjoy.

BROTHER AND SISTER: JAVIER AND JESSICA

MAJOR FEATURES: (JAVIER)

- fine hair
- broad forehead
- high-placed ears
- low-set eyebrows
- eyebrows flat across
- long emotional section
- full cheek area
- left ear comes forward
- balanced lips
- tapered jaw/chin
- rounded chin

CHARACTER ANALYSIS:

Javier is a young man with intelligence (high placed ears and broad forehead) and concern for the welfare of others (fine hair, balanced lips). He has a gentleness expressed in the cheek area and the rounding of the chin, which will make him sensitive to the needs of family and friends. The flat, low-set eyebrows combine to make him easy-going once he knows someone, but he may be somewhat shy at the outset. With his left ear coming forward he probably enjoys lively, festive music (as the base of his nose is broad, not thin like people who enjoy string, classical music). The left and right eye (when the face is split vertically) are different. The left eye, his "inner child side," is much more open and spiritual.

LIFE CHALLENGE(S) AND GROWTH:

For those of us who have long faces with tapered jaws and rounded chin, areas of assertiveness, setting boundaries with others, speaking our needs and being powerful and self-confident are the life lessons.

BROTHER AND SISTER: JAVIER AND JESSICA (cont.)

MAJOR FEATURES: (JESSICA)

- broad forehead
- wispy corners of hairline (not shown in this photo)
- rounded eyebrows
- visible eyelids
- wide-set eyes
- high ears with inner rims turned back
- full cheeks
- wide mouth
- wide jaw, rounded chin
- large front teeth

CHARACTER ANALYSIS:

Jessica is loving (rounded cheeks, rounded eyebrows, wide mouth) and fun to be with (sparkle in eye tone)! She has many close friends (wide mouth and full cheeks) and a special bond with her mother (wispy corners of hairline). Intelligent (high-placed ears and broad forehead), she does well in academics, especially in areas requiring an unusual or creative approach (ear rims turn back on themselves)—writing, abstract math, or projects involving putting people together to accomplish a specific goal. She is action oriented and likes to finish projects she starts (wide jaw and visible eyelids). She gets along well with everyone (wide mouth, rounding of facial features and chin)!

AREAS OF LIFE LESSON(S) OR GROWTH:

Because Jessica's face expresses so much genuine sincerity and sweetness, (her wide-set eyes, wide mouth, full cheeks, bright eye tone, rounded chin), occasionally people may take advantage of her goodness or willingness to be helpful.

WHAT THEY CAN LEARN FROM EACH OTHER:

Javier and Jessica get along very well together even though Jessica is more extroverted and verbal in social settings. Javier has an innate nobility and kindness with inner strength, which will become more and more powerful. Both are intelligent and hard workers, sensitive to the needs of others.

MOTHER AND SON: NANCY AND BEN

In looking at the photos of children, one looks for their natural gifts and tendencies, the goal being to maximize their hidden potentials and minimize their negatives tendencies. At birth some of these gifts will be apparent, and as the child develops, the environment, parental influence, and the child's own life experience will change and develop their face. By looking at the three sections of the face at birth: Forehead (thinking), Cheeks (feeling), Jaw (the body's care), one can note which area is the longest. The longest section will show where they are predominantly focused in their personality. The shortest section will show a part of themselves which they will have to develop to remain balanced as an individual.

MAJOR FEATURES (NANCY):

- high, broad forehead
- rounded hairline
- fine, blonde hair
- arched eyebrows—fine
- wide-set eyes with visible eyelids
- strong nasolabial lines
- no philtrum
- long ear lobes with low ears
- visible gums and large front teeth
- wide mouth with balanced lips
- round chin

CHARACTER ANALYSIS:

A very warm-hearted, (large cheeks, wide-set eyes, large mouth), and sensitive woman, (fine hair shaft), Nancy combines a deep spirituality (long lobes, bright eye tone) with a practical common sense (high, broad forehead). Generosity and caring are very important in her relationships with others (round chin, wide mouth, wide-set eyes). The visible gums suggest one who is also generous financially when others are in need. Her blue eye tint would also suggest one who freely buys books or does experiential work in the spiritual area to expand her concepts and awareness (wide-broad forehead, wide-set eyes, large ear lobes, blue eye color).

A popular person who has many long term friendships (rounded hairline, wide mouth, wide-set eyes), Nancy is very loyal to those close to her (high eyebrows). If challenged by someone who is dishonest or treacherous, her arched eyebrows show that she would flair up to protect her son.

AREAS OF LIFE CHALLENGE OR GROWTH:

The fine eyebrows and lack of philtrum combine as facial features to suggest that at times (like 3:00 p.m.) Nancy might go through energy slumps or have a tendency to drink too much coffee.

Also, as many of the areas of her face suggest her to be loving and freely giving to others, the balance and challenge for her is to find private time to take care of her own spiritual needs and aspirations. Quiet and mental relaxation are key for her both for her peace of mind and also to help her stay healthy. Not always easy for a mom with a toddler!

MAJOR FEATURES (BEN):

- high, broad forehead
- fine, blonde hair
- low eyebrows
- wide-set eye with non-visible eyelids
- high-placed ears which come forward
- short chin and jaw area

CHARACTER ANALYSIS:

Ben will be a brilliant non-conformist with musical ability as he gets older (ears come forward, high, broad forehead). A sensitive and independent child (fine, blonde hair, ears come forward), he will also be a natural leader (broad cheeks indicate self confidence, and low eyebrows indicate friendliness). He will be exacting in nature (non-visible eyelids in a child) but also very loving and big hearted (bright, spiritual blue eyes and large cheeks).

AREAS OF LIFE CHALLENGE OR GROWTH:

With strengths in the mental and spiritual areas, Ben's challenging area will be taking care of his body (short chin and jaw area). He will not be interested in eating a balanced diet or brushing his teeth. He would much rather read a book or play a musical instrument! Ben may also have trouble sleeping deeply through the night (fine hair shaft and short chin area).

MOTHER-SON COMPATIBILITY:

There is a natural flow of love and feeling here with emphasis on the mental and spiritual gifts of each.

- Mental stimulation: Nancy will help Ben by reading with him, developing his creative and intellectual abilities (both have the high, broad foreheads).

85

- Spirituality demonstrated in a practical way towards others: Nancy and Ben will both see the "big" picture when it comes to others and people's strengths and weaknesses, striving to overlook the shortcomings in others (long lobes, full cheeks, wide-set eyes, Ben's low eyebrows matched to Nancy's wide mouth). Ben will learn a lot about friendship, love and genuine nurturing and loyalty from his mother. His creative spirit and intellectual brilliance will blossom.

- Music and play are important: Ben will have natural music ability (ears forward), Nancy's innate tenderness (round chin) will want him to be happy and joyful, helping him to cultivate areas he loves.

LIFE CHALLENGES OR GROWTH AREAS: (Nancy and Ben together)

Especially when Nancy's physical energy is low (no philtrum and fine eyebrows) and when Ben is refusing to brush his teeth (as an example), she might get short tempered (arched eyebrows) or frustrated at his sometimes irregular eating or sleeping habits.

FATHER AND SON: JON AND JONAS

MAJOR FEATURES: (JON, THE FATHER)

- short, rounded forehead
- worry-lines above nose
- low-set eyebrows
- visible eyelids
- small eyes
- long philtrum
- small mouth
- right mouth: self-esteem mark
- balanced lips
- low-set ears with long lobes
- face larger at jaw/chin area

CHARACTER ANALYSIS:

Jon is a humanitarian (rounded, short forehead, low-set eyebrows) who relies on "gut" feelings about people and inner spiritual understanding (long ear lobes). A no-nonsense person when it comes to truth, religion, or humanitarian goals, Jon uses his profession to bring compassion (large cheeks) and practical insight to others in a non-judgmental way (long ear lobes, low-set eyebrows, rounded forehead, balanced lips). Jon is big-hearted (cheek area) but could be dangerous to cross swords with if a situation presented to him were immoral or unethical (small mouth, small eyes).

LIFE CHALLENGE(S) OR GROWTH:

The left eye suggests that Jon is working out issues of family-of-origin sadness. The low ears and self-esteem mark on the right mouth suggest someone who is a late bloomer in finding their life path or vocation, and this at times is challenging financially. Under pressure Jon might become depressed (large cheeks and large lower jaw and chin area) or self-critical (left jaw bigger than the right) especially if he doesn't feel connected to humanity or his own innate spiritual depth.

 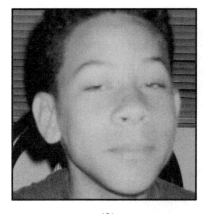 

a (1)   **a (2)**   **b (recent)**

MAJOR FEATURES (JONAS):

Two (a) photos were selected out of five and are shown here. In Jonas's face there were major changes in the last year as expressed in many of his facial features:

Changes:

- (a) rounded hairline became (b) a somewhat square hairline
- (a) high eyebrows became (b) medium eyebrows
- (a) lower placed ear which comes forward became (b) higher ears, which lie against the head
- (a) nostrils fall above the lower ear lobe, and now (b) the nose appears larger and lower
- (a) long philtrum became (b) short philtrum

Other facial features, which remained constant:

- full cheeks
- balanced lips
- narrow chin

CHARACTER ANALYSIS:

What is fascinating about seeing different photos of Jonas is that they are so different! What does it mean when someone's face has changed so markedly?

This is a young man who is going through major life transitions both at school and at home. What do these transitions signify for him?

Whereas he used to be friendly (even brows, rounded forehead) but somewhat shy (high eyebrows, narrow chin), and bored in school, Jonas is becoming more outgoing and more interested in scholastics, applying himself in a dynamic way (square hairline and higher ears in (b)) and getting better grades. His small, even teeth suggest someone who is a quick learner. His full cheek area (generous or warm-hearted) and the square hairline give him a balance for the future of achieving high goals, yet at the same time, making him aware of the needs and feelings of others—a nice balance. His eyebrow height is lowering, making him appear to others to be more available for athletics and activities. It looks like he is coming into his own now!

LIFE CHALLENGE(S) AND GROWTH:

With the lower left jaw being wider than the right side, he could be hard on himself or self-critical when under stress. The combination of the narrow chin (gentle nature or somewhat of an introvert) and the full cheeks (sensitive to the needs of his friends) might make him conform to peer pressure on occasion when he really doesnt want to.

LIFE CHALLENGE(S) AND GROWTH (Jon and Jonas together):

Jon may, from his early life experiences, unknowingly put more pressure than he realizes on Jonas to achieve and "cut a clear path" early in life—maybe too early from Jonas's point of view. Jonas will be sensitive and brilliant in his own area, but considering how radically his face has changed in the last year, he will need lots of space to develop his individuality. He will learn from his father's humanitarian and spiritual strength, even though this may not be verbalized between the two. Jonas will have an agile and lighthearted approach which occasionally will come across as irresponsible, but is really his own developing, creative spirit.

MOTHER AND DAUGHTER: DEBBIE AND ADDIE

MAJOR FEATURES: (DEBBIE, THE MOTHER)

- high, broad forehead
- brown, straight hair
- low-set rounded eyebrows
- narrow bridge of nose
- brown eyes
- full cheeks with strong nasolabial lines
- short philtrum
- no upper lip
- strong, forward chin

CHARACTER ANALYSIS:

Debbie is a dynamic and serious-minded (straight, brown hair, forward chin area) woman who has loving and strong feelings (large cheek area and rounded eyebrows). Her left eye appears more open than the right. This indicates that she has developed an active inner, spiritual life. The nasolabial lines over the cheeks being distinct and the upper lip being thin both indicate that Debbie has had to teach herself how to communicate her deepest feelings, to learn to ask for what she needs emotionally, and to negotiate situations involving angry or difficult people.

Her broad, high forehead and full cheeks, with joyful eyes and low-set, rounded eyebrows reveal a professional who combines intellectual insight with a genuine heart quality. Her daughter and family are of prime importance in her life (brown hair, brown eyes), and she is a wonderful mother to Addie.

LIFE LESSON(S) OR GROWTH:

The upper bridge of the nose being narrow suggests a person who needs quiet time to recharge emotionally and physically. If she did not get this, she might become a perfectionist (the same facial feature under stress) and lose her usual spiritual overview and humor.

The corresponding verbal statement expressed on her face would be: "So much to do! So little time!" Any extra time she has would be devoted to her daughter or husband, and it is important that she also have quiet time on her own everyday.

MOTHER AND DAUGHTER: DEBBIE AND ADDIE (cont.)

MAJOR FEATURES: (ADDIE, THE DAUGHTER)

- large, wide forehead
- straight, light brown hair
- fine hair shaft
- low-set eyebrows
- hazel eyes
- high-placed ears
- long ear lobes
- full, beautiful cheeks
- thin upper lip
- strong nasolabial lines
- wide jaw

CHARACTER ANALYSIS:

Naturally popular and friendly (low-set eyebrows, full cheeks), Addie will also excel at school (high-placed ears and high, broad forehead) having an agile and inquiring mind (hazel eyes). She will be a balance of sweetness (fine hair shaft, large cheeks) and strong will power (strong jaw area). The sensitive feeling expressed in her face combined with her hazel eyes will make her someone who will want to understand people from the inside-out, their thoughts, their feelings, why they behave like they do.

Her even and rounded eyebrows will indicate that she will like friendships to be harmonious and will be eager to make them flow smoothly. Her long ear lobes also suggest innate wisdom and an understanding of life beyond her years.

LIFE LESSON(S) AND GROWTH:

The thin upper lip and strong nasolabial lines suggest someone who will need to be encouraged to appropriately express her anger and negative feelings when they arise.

MOTHER-DAUGHTER COMPATIBILITY:

What is so wonderful in this relationship is that Debbie (the mother) has learned to feel and express in a loving and yet dynamic way her feelings and emotions. Addie (the daughter) with her hazel eyes and sensitive, tender features will grow and learn from her mother how to understand people of varied backgrounds and how to maneuver in the professional world, keeping one's heart honest and open. For Debbie, Addie's natural charm and brightness will be a joy. Her mental quickness mentally will make her receptive to creative and fun projects which the two of them will do together.

LIFE LESSON(S) OR GROWTH:

Both Debbie and Addie have the "emotional" area as predominant in their faces, which means both will continually be learning how to nuture themselves and create private time for themselves to relax and rejuvenate. Also, they will both learn from each other how to speak their "truth"— especially when it conflicts with others's opinions and the status quo.

MARRIAGE COMPATIBILITY: JOE AND DOLORES

High School

Recent

MAJOR FEATURES: (JOE)

- large, wide forehead
- one line above nose
- low eyebrows
- "teacher lines"
- in-set eyes with brightness
- full cheeks
- large front teeth with balanced lips
- ears with long lobes; ears' inner rim turns back on itself
- "Artisan" beard and mustache

CHARACTER ANALYSIS:

Friendly and open (low-set eyes with even gaze), Joe is a spiritual seeker (in-set eyes with long ear lobes and inner rim of ears turns back on itself), interested in areas of personal growth and transformation. He had to go in a completely different direction emotionally and spiritually than his family (one vertical line above the nose). His "teacher lines" on both the right and left indicate his love of communication and his occupation, a college professor. With the spiritual depth shown in the five areas of his face, it is important for Joe also to inspire others and encourage them in their inner growth and transformation. Strong, clear, horizontal forehead lines with a large, open forehead reveal his clear thinking ability coupled with an innate kindness and feeling (the large cheeks). Joe's close-set eyes with "Artisan" beard and mustache reveal a man who pays attention to detail and enjoys working with his hands (carpentry, art, etc).

AREAS OF LIFE CHALLENGE(S) OR GROWTH:

Because responsibility, accountability, and service to others are major themes in his face, were he to delegate a project to someone who did not follow-through or let Joe know the project was left unfinished, this would be particularly frustrating to him. Although friendly by nature and a man who can get along with a wide variety of personalities, Joe needs to be with people who are also actualizing their creative potential, or he would get bored.

MARRIAGE COMPATIBILITY: JOE AND DOLORES (cont.)

College

Recent

MAJOR FEATURES (DOLORES):

- large, wide forehead
- square hairline (early photo)
- non-visible eyelids
- close-set eyes
- medium height eyebrows
- "teacher lines" and "crow's feet" along outer eyelids
- round eyebrows with flat outer edge
- narrow base of nose
- balanced lips
- large front teeth
- forward thrusting chin

CHARACTER ANALYSIS:

A woman with a high intellect (high forehead, high ears), Dolores has tremendous energy (square hairline) for her teaching work ("teacher lines"). Good with details (close-set eyes) and a planner and list maker (non-visible eyelids), she has an organized and strong willed approach to whatever the task is at hand (large front teeth, chin comes forward). Her tint of blue eye color suggests someone who lives high principles and will fight for what she feels is right. Basically harmonious in working with others (rounded eyebrows, balanced lips), she needs some private time to recharge all she gives out to others (narrow base of nose, flat outer edge of eyebrows). She would probably be drawn to classical music—strings or something soothing (her full cheeks and narrow base of the nose) like Beethoven or Vivaldi. Her beautiful cheek structure suggests someone with humor ("crow's feet") and an innate kindness.

AREAS OF LIFE CHALLENGE(S) OR GROWTH:

Dolores' face reflects so much generosity and giving of herself to others, that taking time out to nurture herself will be important. It may be difficult for her at times to slow down her pace and also to say "no" to the many offers of new and interesting creative projects she will continually receive.

SIMILAR FEATURES: (8)   (85%+) — Very compatible!

- High-wide foreheads: Intellectual understanding and creativity is important to both of them.

- Same eye shape: They "see" the world is similar ways in terms of ethics and values.

- Eye color is mutable (grey to blue) on both: Very flexible people.

- Noses similar with left upper eyebrow higher than right: Money has gone up and down during the marriage, especially early on, and both have worked to help each other with this.

- Both have full cheeks: Feelings and being sensitive to the needs of the other is important.

- Hair shaft is fine: Both have developed sensitivity and an appreciation of quality.

- Balanced lips on both: They both like to balance giving and receiving in their relationship, although Dolores might do more projects on the physical plane (the house or organizing with children) than Joe.

- "Teacher lines": Communication and the arts are important to both, and they have a common profession (teaching).

DISSIMILAR FEATURES: (2)

- They have different forehead lines. Joe's two horizontal lines cross the forehead and one vertical line goes vertically from the base of the nose. Dolores has two vertical lines between her eyebrows.

- The eyebrow height (from the eyes) is different: Joe has low-set eyebrows and Dolores' eyebrows are medium set.

AREAS OF LIFE CHALLENGE(S) OR GROWTH:

Dolores' high square forehead and high energy keep her going long hours after her professional day is over. Joe prefers more solitude and inner meditation (long lobes, ear rim turned back) after a long day. In religious preference, Dolores' eye color of blue indicates a more traditional approach than Joe's, but both have inner depth and spiritual understanding.

MARRIAGE COMPATIBILITY: JON AND THERESE

MAJOR FEATURES: (THERESE)

- large, high rounded forehead
- thick hair shaft
- low-set eyebrows
- wide-set eyes
- "crow's feet" at eyes
- nasolabial lines around the mouth area
- wide mouth with balanced lips
- large front teeth
- low-placed ears
- strong jaw and chin

CHARACTER ANALYSIS:

Therese is a high energy, (strong jaw & chin) very intelligent (very large, wide forehead) woman with a strong humanitarian heart (rounded forehead, clear eye tone, wide mouth, wide-set eyes). It is important for her to be working for the "Big" picture of spirituality and world peace (large cheeks, wide-set eyes). Highly verbal (nasolabial lines which circle the mouth area), she has definite opinions about spiritual and world issues, (wide-set eyes with strong chin and large front teeth.) The low-set eyebrows and her wide mouth make her easily likeable, and others find her both loving (cheek structure, rounded forehead) and inspiring.

Her balanced face sections give her face a sincere common sense approach to life. She is able to move forward in achieving her goals and the goals of her family, which are very important to her (left cheek wider than right.) Her low ears with the inner rims turned backwards indicate a late bloomer and also a woman who easily blends practicality, creativity, and new and original ways of thinking (grey-blue eyes).

LIFE CHALLENGE(S) OR GROWTH:

With all the parts of Therese's face showing such a dynamic person, petty politics or insignificant differences between people might drive her crazy! If others are irresponsible or unethical, Therese's face shows the compassion (cheek area, rounded hairline) to feel for their situation, but this might be a challenge for her.

MARRIAGE COMPATIBILITY: JON AND THERESE (cont.)

MAJOR FEATURES: (JON)

- short, rounded forehead
- worry-lines above nose
- low-set eyebrows
- visible eyelids
- small eyes
- long philtrum
- small mouth
- right mouth: self-esteem mark
- balanced lips
- low-set ears with long lobes
- face larger at jaw/chin area

CHARACTER ANALYSIS:

Jon's rounded, short forehead indicates a humanitarian (low-set eyebrows) who relies on "gut" feelings about people and inner spiritual understanding (long ear lobes.) A no-nonsense person when it comes to truth, religion, humanitarian goals, he uses his profession to bring compassion (large cheeks) and practical insight to others in a very non-judgmental way (long ear lobes, low-set eyebrows, rounded forehead, balanced lips). Jon is big-hearted (cheek area) but could be dangerous to cross swords with if the situation presented to him were immoral or unethical (small eyes, small mouth).

LIFE CHALLENGE(S) OR GROWTH:

The left eye suggests that Jon is working out issues of family-of-origin sadness. The low ears and self-esteem mark on the right mouth suggest someone who is a late bloomer in finding their life path or vocation. This at times can be challenging financially! Under pressure Jon might become depressed (large cheeks and large lower jaw and chin area) or self-critical (left jaw bigger than the right) especially if he doesn't feel connected to humanity or his own innate spiritual depth.

MARRIAGE COMPATIBILITY: (90%+)—Very compatible!

SIMILAR FEATURES: (9)

- Rounded hairlines: They both are friendly, spiritual and perhaps musical. They both have many friendships which have lasted for years.

- Broad foreheads: Both think in "Big" terms, focusing on the universal good and spiritual ideals.

- Low-set eyebrows: Both are easy to get to know and affable.

- Flat lid area under eye: The quality here of being cautious or wary in first meeting people is softened by the other facial features of wide-set eyes and rounded forehead. Put together, the flat lower lid acts then to give them "grounding" and a common sense to relationships.

- Full cheeks: Love and sensitivity to the other's needs is stressed in their family life.

- Low ears (see other photo, close-up of Jon): Both are late-bloomers, coming into their full power between the ages of 30-40.

- Large front teeth: Both are strong-willed people!

- Balanced lips: In their marriage, they both give and receive, knowing that balance is important for healthy relationships.

- Strong jaw and chin area: Again, both have strong drive and will-power. At times when Jon gets discouraged, he might lean towards depression.

DISSIMILAR FEATURES: (2)

- Therese's tall forehead; Jon's short forehead: Therese might have more formal academic education than Jon, whose gifts are in the intuitive and a very quick under-standing of other's motives and personalities. They learn and draw from each other in this way.

- Therese eye color blue-gray; Jon's eye color brown: Therese's eye color reveals a humanitarian with quick analytical skills. Jon's brown eye color suggests a man who is serious-minded and family oriented.

SUMMARY: Both Therese and Jon are strong-willed, strong feeling individuals who share a spiritual overview and humanitarian ideals. They are generous, and giving in their relationship and with their children.

At times Jon's intuitive and spiritual guidance conflict with the financial planning or security of the family, so Therese is a perfect person for him as she understands the Divine Plan and Jon's deep faith. Consequently, things will always work out for them on the material plane.

Part VI
Epilogue

EPILOGUE

Face Reading helps us to deeply understand people who might otherwise appear to us as strangers. With the techniques of Face Reading, we can now look at them and see from their faces both their gifts and their shortcomings. My hope is that the insights gained through this healing tool will deepen the understanding, love, and compassion we have for ourselves and others.

ABOUT THE AUTHOR

Barbara Roberts has appeared as a monthly guest on KGTV's *InSide San Diego*, and has made several special appearances on the *Channel 9 Morning News*, Southwestern and Cox Cable programs, and AM 1000's radio talk shows.

A registered nurse with a background in clinical medical research, Barbara has been a guest speaker and staff-trainer at major medical centers and colleges throughout San Diego, training over 2000 people in areas of holistic healing. Her expertise in clinical assessment led her to author a nationally distributed medical manual, *Medical Assessment Skills*. Ms. Roberts is co-author of nationally recognized papers and abstracts in OB/GYN, and she was the co-recipient of the 1983 Hewing Medical Award for research. She graduated Phi Beta Kappa and Magna Cum Laude with a Bachelor of Arts degree in Social Psychology from Case-Western Reserve University.

Searching for a system of understanding people that was both scientific and intuitive, Barbara discovered the ancient system of Face Reading. Studying first under Dr. Narayan Singh, psychologist and internationally recognized teacher and author, Ms. Roberts has developed her own unique Face Reading style. She currently lives in the San Diego area where she teaches Face Reading classes, offers business consulting, and conducts sessions for individuals and couples.

For more information, or if you wish a <u>personal Face Reading</u>, (see following page), please write to her care of:

Barbara Roberts
c/o Face Reading #227
1106 Second Street
Encinitas, CA 92024

Dr. Narayan Singh says of her ability:

"Barbara Roberts has become perhaps the most effective Face Reader I have encountered in my travels. She is a Face Reader par excellence, and a person of great compassion, sensitivity, and commitment."

INTRODUCTORY OFFER!

HOW TO GET YOUR <u>OWN</u> PERSONAL FACE READING

A 40-MINUTE <u>CASSETTE</u> WITH DETAILED
INTERPRETATION OF <u>YOUR</u> FACE!

"Barbara has a tremendous healing gift in the individual Face Reading sessions. This was the single most important step I took in understanding my true inner self."

> *Ruth Barry*
> *San Diego, CA*

"I have watched Barbara look at pictures of people she's never met nor seen before, and identify their exact personality traits with complete accuracy. For me, this information has proven invaluable."

> *Nancy Johnson*
> *Encinitas, CA*

"Barbara's rare gifts of insight and her wonderful sense of humor provide her students a most valuable lesson in self-awarness, self-acceptance, and joy. I have found her work most helpful in my own life and practice."

> *Martha Odegaard*
> *La Jolla, CA*

Face Reading is an accurate, introspective tool for helping us understand ourselves and the true natures of those around us. The goal of Face Reading is mental and emotional healing through insight. Though Face Reading is not a substitute for professional counseling, it offers one valuable glimpses into who we are and why others respond to us as they do.

In your taped Face Reading session, I will explore both your inner gifts and talents along with areas for personal growth and change. As you listen to comments on unfinished areas within your life, please be gentle with yourself and realize these may take time to change and heal. As we do our inner work, changing from within, our faces will reflect this recovery and growth. Occasionally, the facial features may not yet have responded to issues which you feel you have already addressed and healed, so please don't be discouraged.

To receive your Individual Face Reading please send the following:

1) <u>Three **color close-up photos**</u> showing your hairline, ears and a smile! You might pull your hair back and put it behind your ears. Include one photo in profile if you can. The <u>larger</u> the photo, the better!

2) <u>A check or money order</u> (no cash please) for **$65.00** and your name, street address, city, state and zip code, work and home phone numbers (with area code.)

You will receive a 40-minute cassette tape analysis of your face, sent to you by first class mail. The price includes tax, shipping and handling. A padded envelope to protect your photos will be provided. Photos will not be returned by certified or registered mail, so please do not send "one-of-a-kind" photos (in case they are lost or damaged in the mail). You might want to make **color photocopies** of them at a local copier store and keep the originals.

**Special offer for readers of this 1st Edition: Orders for Individual Face Readings must be received by July, 1995 to honor the Introductory price of $65 for the 40-minute tape.

3) <u>**Make out check or money order for $65 and mail to:**</u>

> **Barbara Roberts**
> **Face Reading #227**
> **1106 Second Street**
> **Encinitas, CA 92024**

(Due to numerous orders, please allow up to 3 weeks for your tape).

May your personal reading bring you both healing and insight!

My best to you!

Sincerely,

Barbara

Barbara Roberts
#227-1106 2nd St.
Encinitas, CA 92024
(619) 944-1460